# AUTOMATING APARTHEID –

## U.S. COMPUTER EXPORTS TO SOUTH AFRICA AND THE ARMS EMBARGO

NARMIC/American Friends Service Committee

NARMIC is a program of the American Friends Service Committee. NARMIC Staff: Thomas Conrad, Eva Gold, David Goodman, Mary Morrell; NARMIC Interns: Susan Benner, Rebekah Ray-Crichton, Marilyn Wood.

*Automating Apartheid* is published in cooperation with the United Methodist Church Board of Global Ministries and the World Campaign Against Military and Nuclear Collaboration with South Africa. Project Director: Thomas Conrad. Design and layout: Eliza Drake. Printing: Omega Press, Philadelphia.

Copies of *Automating Apartheid* are available from NARMIC, 1501 Cherry Street, Philadelphia, PA 19102.

**PRICES**

**Nonprofit Institutions and Individuals**
  *1-9 copies*: $3.50 each plus 50¢ postage and handling for domestic orders (for overseas orders, add $1.50 for postage and handling);
  *10 or more copies*: 40 percent discount (no returns); NARMIC will pay postage and handling on prepaid orders.

**Corporations and Others**
  *1-9 copies*: $10 each plus 50¢ postage and handling for domestic orders (for overseas orders, add $1.50 for postage and handling);
  *10 or more copies*: 20 percent discount (no returns); NARMIC will pay postage and handling on prepaid orders.

# CONTENTS

# FOREWORD

NARMIC has broken new ground with *Automating Apartheid* by ferreting out links between U.S. corporations and Pretoria that have never seen the light of day. This report is a vital new contribution to the public debate on U.S. involvement in South Africa. *Automating Apartheid* gives a closeup look at the way advanced U.S. technology enables the racist policy of apartheid to be implemented with a high degree of precision.

How important is high-tech equipment from the United States to Pretoria? As this new study helps to show, U.S. corporations are outfitting apartheid's practicioners with the very tools they need to implement, maintain and defend this inhuman system. White-ruled South Africa has compensated for its lack of sufficient personnel to run the apartheid system by relying on the resources of a vast array of computers and electronics from U.S. corporations. This study shows that the only major U.S. policy taken in opposition to apartheid – the arms embargo – has been seriously subverted and, in fact, has been made a mockery.

Computers and high-tech exports represent but one part of a total of $2.6 billion of U.S. investment in South Africa. It is virtually impossible to control how any U.S. products are used once they reach South Africa. As long as sales of advanced technology to South Africa continue, we must assume that Pretoria will use it for strategic and repressive purposes. At the very least, further investment by U.S. firms in data processing products in South Africa should be firmly prohibited.

Time in South Africa is surely running out and when it does, the quality of American relations with that country–including the impact of those relations on the black majority – will be held up to scrutiny. Sooner or later, we will be judged as to whether we conducted our affairs with South Africa in a way which enhanced the participation of the majority population in their society. We will be judged as to whether we were on the right side of freedom, or partners in the crime of racism.

William Gray, III
U.S. House of Representatives

# PREFACE

The same U.S. corporations that have desegregated the lunchrooms in their South African facilities as a result of public pressure in the United States are still outfitting the Pretoria government with advanced computers, electronic components and other sophisticated technology. Although pressure on U.S. corporations doing business in South Africa has increased dramatically over the past ten years, much of the debate has focused on the companies' employment practices. In response to public criticism, Reverend Leon Sullivan and other leaders developed a business code of conduct, calling for the desegregation of U.S. corporate facilities in South Africa and pressing for fair treatment of blacks. The "Sullivan Principles," as they have come to be called, have received strong support from the U.S. government, won acclaim in business circles, and have been emulated by corporations in other countries.

Although the Sullivan Principles have been hailed by some activists as a step in the right direction, they have done little to change the structural causes of oppression in South Africa. Moreover, much of the discussion of the employment code, and the effort devoted to monitoring the signators' compliance with it, have tended to channel public attention away from one of the most critical aspects of U.S. corporate involvement in South Africa: the strategic value of products and services available from U.S. corporations, and their availability to the white-controlled government, the military and key sectors of South Africa's industry. Anyone seeking to understand the full scope and significance of U.S. corporate support for apartheid cannot afford to overlook this central issue. By focusing on transfers of high technology (or in the trade language, "high-tech"), we hope to widen this debate and stimulate further investigation.

Solid information about U.S. corporate operations in South Africa is hard to come by. For the most part, details about military contracting and sales to the South African government are simply not divulged. The disclosure of any business information outside the country is subject to Pretoria's approval. The home offices of U.S. corporations with subsidiaries in South Africa are not eager to have their foreign operations scrutinized. Many of the companies NARMIC staff contacted as part of our inquiry declined to provide us with any information. A few supplied cautious replies to some of our questions.

In addition to restrictions on the flow of information from South Africa, and the reticence of U.S. corporations, our research was made difficult by the erosion of the Freedom of Information Act. Early on in this project, NARMIC sought the release of export licenses granted by the Commerce and State Departments to U.S. corporations, authorizing the sale of high-tech equipment to South African end-users. Despite the intent of the Act, the government has moved to make export licenses automatically exempt from release. This new measure protects the identity of U.S. companies trading with repressive governments around the world, and, sadly, it prevents the public from knowing the full scope and impact of these exports. NARMIC also asked the State Department to release several documents concerning the U.S. government's effort to monitor the South Africans' compliance with the arms embargo. This request was also turned down.

Despite these setbacks, a wealth of other material was obtained under the Freedom of Information Act for this study, much of which is cited in the text and notes. In addition to these sources, we made extensive use of the few published materials available in South Africa that do provide information about the use of technology and U.S. exports. These include government publications such as the Defence White Papers, the military magazines, *Paratus, Armed Forces,* the police magazine, *Servamus,* as well as the *State Tender Bulletin* and reports from the Council for Scientific and Industrial Research. Among the other sources of information we found particularly helpful are *Electronics and Instrumentation, Management* and *Security and Protection of SA.*

The bulk of the sales of high-tech equipment cited here involve transactions that are known to have occurred. Given the South Africans' penchant for secrecy and the fact that Pretoria is known to be stockpiling electronic equipment, the sales we have spotlighted in this study undoubtedly represent only the tip of the iceberg. Going beyond this point necessarily involves speculation. We have speculated about probable and potential sales of U.S.-origin technology and its uses only when circumstantial evidence warrants it, and we have taken care to indicate where this is the case.

A number of people and organizations have enriched our work immeasurably with generous contributions of time and resources. We are happy to express our thanks to them here. Others who were involved cannot be named but we wish to acknowledge their help with deep gratitude.

Special thanks are due to Susan Benner, NARMIC's intern who assembled a list of South African computer installations and devoted many hours of other careful work to the project. We are also grateful to Jim Hewitt, who compiled the corporate profiles; to the NARMIC Advisory Committee for help and encouragement; to our friends on AFSC staff and committees and others who read and commented on the manuscript; to Walter Schenck, Isaac Bivens and Kassahun Checole for helpful advice and support, and to David Rudovsky, Susan DeJarnatt, Philip O'Neill and David Vladek for legal advice.

In addition, we express our deep appreciation to Abdul Minty, Director of the World Campaign Against Military and Nuclear Collaboration with South Africa; Jennifer Davis of the American Committee on Africa; to Tim Smith of the Interfaith Center for Corporate Responsibility; to the Washington Office on Africa; the United Nations Centre Against Apartheid; the Anti-Apartheid Movement in the United Kingdom; Sami Faltas; the Dutch Anti-Apartheids Beweging; Bill Anderson; the Transnational Institute; the West German Anti-Apartheid Bewegung; the Stichting Onderzoek Multinationale Concernen; Kairos; the Moore School Library of the University Pennsylvania and the Library of Congress.

In addition to their support for this work, the Board of Global Ministries of the United Methodist Church has helped fund NARMIC's research as well as the publication of this study. We are particularly grateful to the African Affairs Program of the World Division and the Education and Cultivation Division. NARMIC also acknowledges with deep gratitude grants toward this project made by the World Campaign Against Military and Nuclear Collaboration with South Africa, the Programme to Combat Racism of the World Council of Churches and the Marianist Sharing Fund.

Note: 1 Rand is the approximate equivalent of U.S. $1.04.

# CHAPTER ONE

## INTRODUCTION:
## THE ROOTS OF APARTHEID

Nowhere is racism more blatant, pervasive and institutionally established than in South Africa. Racial separation and white supremacy are the twin pillars of Pretoria's social order. They are implemented by government agencies, defended by the internal security forces and ultimately backed by an arsenal of high technology, much of which is willingly supplied by U.S. corporations. This study identifies some of the companies involved in this trade and examines how their products and services streamline and bolster the apartheid system.

The abhorence of the international community for apartheid took concrete form in 1963 when the members of the United Nations passed an embargo on military sales to South Africa. In 1977, the embargo became mandatory, and in 1978 the United States extended the ban to cover all sales — not only sales of arms — to Pretoria's policy and military. Despite these controls and despite the minority government's resistance to change, U.S. corporations have continued to sell, lease and maintain computers and other technology which support government, police and military operations in South Africa.

The volume of this trade shows every sign of increasing as the Reagan Administration relaxes the arms embargo and signals its intention of improving relations with the white minority regime. One indication of the United States' growing tilt toward Pretoria came into clear view in October of 1981 when the U.S. government approved the export of a sophisticated Sperry Univac computer to Atlas Aircraft, a state-owned weapons-maker.[1] Ironically, a few weeks later, the Reagan Administration turned down a request from the Mennonite Central Committee for permission to send pencils and rulers to school children in Kampuchea. The Commerce Department initially told the Mennonite relief agency that the school supplies could be construed as developmental aid and thus a violation of U.S. policy to prevent the export of anything that might strengthen the Kampuchean government, a position which has since been somewhat relaxed. By contrast, the Univac computer destined for Atlas Aircraft will bolster a military machine that has been condemned around the world for its brutality and aggression.

*Children behind fence that separates them from a white area near Johannesburg. United Nations/Pendl*

## The Roots of Apartheid

What is the nature of South Africa's apartheid system, which the U.S. Administration seems increasingly willing to ignore? With sweeping powers vested in the central government and a web of repressive laws, the white minority in South Africa controls over eighty percent of the population. Most black Africans are considered citizens of the "bantustans" or "homelands" — some of the most unproductive and marginal land in South Africa. In theory Africans living in the homelands are supposed to be self-sufficient but the low productivity of the land, overcrowding and lack of opportunity all make this impossible. The per capita income in the homelands is about one-fifteenth that of the rest of South Africa.[2] In 1980, about 30,000 African children across South Africa were estimated to have died of starvation. Many others have died from related diseases and weakness caused by malnutrition.[3]

Conditions in the homelands force millions of Africans to migrate to white areas to find employment. The minority government strictly controls the movement of African workers into urban areas. Africans are regarded as "migratory citizens" outside the homelands. For the most part, they are allowed to stay in urban areas only if they are employed through a government labor bureau. They are prohibited from owning property.

The "security" of South Africa is insured by some fifty-nine separate laws, passed since 1948, which give Pretoria broad powers to crush dissent. Legislation on the books permits security forces to arrest anyone who opposes the government or is believed to be a terrorist. It enables the government to detain arrestees for 180 days without trial and provides for the declaration of a state of emergency when necessary.[4]

Apartheid is an institutionalized economic, political and social system based on race, which concentrates power in white hands and reduces blacks and Asians to a well regulated supply of cheap labor. The impossibility of survival in the homelands forces workers to accept any wage that is offered. For those who find jobs in urban areas, the ever-present threat of arrest and deportation makes agitation for better conditions or higher wages a dangerous activity. One worker can always be replaced from the vast supply of others desperate for a job, no matter how low the pay is and how bad the working conditions are. Estimates place the unemployment rate among the blacks at twenty to twenty-five percent.[5]

Some changes have occurred in South Africa, prompting claims that the apartheid system is being dismantled.[6] A few of the petty apartheid regulations have been relaxed and some public facilities have been desegregated by special permission. Some trade union rights have been extended to include workers of all races. Over the years, a black middle class has begun to emerge. These developments, however, have done little to change fundamental power relationships.

---

*The "security" of South Africa is insured by some fifty-nine separate laws passed since 1948 which give Pretoria broad powers to crush dissent.*

---

The white regime still maintains control over the lives of the black and Asian majority, determining where they live, whether and under what conditions they work, and, ultimately, whether they live or die.

### U.S. Stakes and Reagan Administration Policies

Two predominant features of the Reagan Administration's policy relating to Pretoria are to pave the way for "a future in which South Africa returns to a place within the regional framework of Western Security interests," and to extend economic ties between the two countries. Briefing papers prepared for the visit to the United States of South African Foreign Minister Pik Botha in May of 1981 indicate that improving relations with Pretoria "represents an obvious opportunity to counter the Soviet threat in Africa;" restoring South Africa's legitimacy in the eyes of the world community would enhance the role South Africa can play in the future as a loyal U.S. ally.[7]

Furthermore, the Reagan Administration views the United States as being locked in a crucial struggle with the Soviet Union for control of the world's strategic minerals and resources. South Africa is the world's fourth largest producer of non-fuel minerals; other southern African nations have significant mineral reserves as well. In an interview televised early in 1981, President Reagan asked, "Can we abandon the country that has stood beside us in every war we've fought, a country that strategically is essential to the free world? It has production of minerals we all must have . . . "[8] In addition to its own wealth of mineral deposits, South Africa occupies a strategic position vis-a-vis the sea lanes through the Indian Ocean and around the South African Cape, which oil bound for the United States must pass.

Nor has South Africa's control over minerals and strategic geographic position escaped the attention of the Pentagon. U.S. military production absorbs a sizable chunk of critical non-fuel minerals, particularly Vanadium and Chromium from South Africa. With drastic increases planned in the military budget for the coming years, the Pentagon will be an even larger consumer of strategic minerals. "We are involving ourselves more aggressively in the raw materials area because it is affecting us so severely," said one U.S. military official.[9]

While the U.S. interest in South African minerals is substantial, the presence of at least 350 U.S.-owned companies in South Africa is the most tangible indication of the U.S. stake in that country. During the past several years, U.S. corporate investment in South Africa has grown enormously, doubling between 1969 and 1974.[10] By the end of 1979, the U.S. stake in South Africa totalled over 2 billion dollars.[11] Increasing U.S. investment in South Africa is tied to the apartheid structure. The pool of cheap labor along with the protection of U.S. interests by the Pretoria government help to make investment in South Africa extremely attractive. Under the Reagan Administration, investment in South Africa is likely to accelerate.

Serious questions are being raised about both the perceptions and the objectives of the Reagan Southern Africa policy. Some critics question the basis of Administration fears of Soviet capability or interest in taking over sea lanes around South Africa. A recent Congressional study counters the idea that South African minerals are essential to western economic well being, and there is no evidence that the supply of minerals or oil would be suspended if majority rule were to be achieved. The United States presently maintains substantial trade with and investment in Zimbabwe despite that country's recent shift to majority rule. U.S. oil companies are even active in Angola, despite the country's marxist orientation.[12]

There is nothing to suggest that democratic rule in South Africa will pose a threat to the United States or its people. The struggle in South Africa is for justice and majority rule, both aspirations embedded in our own heritage and shared by our people. The Reagan Administration's rhetoric of stridency and willingness to overlook oppression in South Africa are more out of place in the 1980s than they have ever been. The world is changing. To view change in South Africa or elsewhere simplistically as a function of U.S.-Soviet conflict is to ignore the complexities of international relations, and the pressing need for liberation.

*Children in their new "homeland," Kwa-Zulu. United Nations/Raynor*

# CHAPTER TWO

# PROGRAMMING OPPRESSION— U.S. COMPUTER COMPANIES IN SOUTH AFRICA

Shortly after the United States tightened controls on exports to South Africa in 1978, a South African business analyst explained why computers are Pretoria's Achilles' Heel. "No other sector of the economy is as utterly dependent as the computer industry is on the multinationals . . . it is a sector through which a stranglehold can be applied on the whole economy," warned the specialist in an article entitled, "How To Beat A Computer Siege."[1]

Of the dozens of data processing companies in South Africa, none do more business than the group of U.S.-owned computer corporations that make up the backbone of the data processing industry there. U.S. computer corporations are not simply implicated in the development of this strategic sector, as are all the foreign high-tech firms in South Africa; they virtually *control* the South African computer market, a function which allies them with the apartheid apparatus, and involves them in the maintenance of minority rule.

The growth of the computer age in South Africa has been closely linked to the consolidation and expansion of the white power structure. Pretoria was quick to recognize the value of the computer for automating government operations and controlling the population. IBM-South Africa received its first order for an "electronic tabulator" in 1952 from the Division of Economics.[2] By 1955, Pretoria had automated its population register with imported hardware, streamlining the hated pass system, which is used to keep tabs on the black majority.[3]

Dozens of other state departments, white-owned industries and financial institutions started installing imported computer hardware in the '50s and '60s. South Africa's military establishment also recognized the value of computer technology and began to automate its operations. In the '60s, the South African Air Force bought foreign-made digital computers and other imported advanced equipment to upgrade its entire air defense system.[4] The first proposal to establish a computer association came from two officials of the African Explosives and Chemical Industry, a large local munitions maker.[5]

Today there are over 4,500 computers installed in South Africa — most of them from the United States.[6] By the beginning of 1980, a South African computer industry survey showed that U.S.-owned corporations sold 75 percent of all the computers in the country, and handled 77 percent of all the local rentals.[7] U.S. data processing companies in South Africa pay R21 million in corporate taxes to Pretoria annually and generate another R11 million in sales tax every year.[8]

Despite pressure from opponents of apartheid, U.S. computer companies have solidified their commitments to South Africa and business is booming. IBM, the largest data processing company in the world, is also the largest computer supplier in South Africa, with total annual sales estimated at R300 million.[9] During 1978 alone, IBM's South African sales jumped by 250 percent.[10] Of the company's workforce, which numbers 1,500, less than twenty percent fall into the officially defined categories of coloureds, blacks or Asians.[11] South Africa's apartheid government is IBM's biggest single customer, accounting for approximately one-third of the company's South African sales.[12]

Burroughs Corporation, the second largest U.S. computer company in South Africa, is estimated to control 17 percent of the local market.[13] Burroughs markets a wide variety of hardware which includes large high-speed central processing units, small and medium-scale computers and facsimile transmission equipment. Like IBM, Burroughs is a major supplier of the government. In 1978,

*By the beginning of 1980, a South African computer industry survey showed that U.S.-owned corporations sold 75 percent of all the computers in the country and handled 77 percent of all the local rentals.*

the company installed the largest computer center in the southern hemisphere for a South African government agency.[14] Burroughs' South African sales increased by 45 percent in 1979.[15]

The third largest U.S. computer company in South Africa is NCR Corporation which supplemented its line of hardware in 1979 with a new series of advanced computers. NCR's revenues in South Africa grew by 16 percent in 1978.[16]

Sperry Univac is the fourth and Control Data Corporation the fifth largest computer subsidiary in South Africa. Several other U.S. corporations in this sector have South African subsidiaries, including Mohawk Data Science, Hewlett Packard, Computer Sciences Corporation, Sperry Rand, 3M, Kodak and Tran Systems.[17]

### "South Africanizing"

Many U.S. high-tech corporations choose not have subsidiaries in South Africa to avoid public relations problems at home. According to a local business journal, "One way out of the dilemma facing multinationals in South Africa is to find a local company to go into partnership with, thus lowering the foreign company's profile here."[18] Dozens of U.S. firms have "South Africanized" and operate through South African distributors (see the appendices for a list of U.S. corporations operating through distributors and agents).

For example, the $200-million-a-year U.S. minicomputer company, Wang Laboratories, "withdrew" from South Africa, leaving its sales to be managed by a locally-owned firm.[19] Wang is now able to claim that it doesn't have a direct subsidiary in South Africa. Yet sales of Wang equipment in South Africa have been increasing by 45 percent every year. "Far from hurting us, I feel the withdrawal has probably strengthened us in the South African marketplace," said a representative of the company's South African distributor.[20]

In order to reduce its dependency on overseas suppliers, the South African government has begun to encourage local production of some electronic components and computer peripheral equipment. However, Pretoria is still overwhelmingly dependent on imported technology: All the large computer mainframes, the vast majority of the hardware in the mid- and mini-range, as well as most peripheral equipment, such as terminals and printers, come from outside the country — most of it from U.S. suppliers.

### Restrictions on U.S. Exports to South Africa

In 1977, after joining the United Kingdom and France in vetoing proposals for more comprehensive economic and military sanctions against South Africa, the United States voted with the majority of the members of the United Nations to make the existing voluntary arms embargo against South Africa mandatory. Yet arms continued to slip into South Africa. During 1977, the State Department approved the export of $4.7 million of military goods on the U.S. Munitions List to South Africa.[21]

The following year, in the wake of international protest which followed the death Steve Biko in a South African jail, Washington extended U.S. controls on sales to South Africa. In February of 1978, the U.S. Commerce Department banned the export of all U.S.-origin products destined for the South African police or military. The new restrictions, which were published as part of the comprehensive *Export Administration Regulations*, appeared to signal a tilt away from South Africa.[22] The government ban was interpreted to cover not only the South African police and military, but also ARMSCOR, the state-owned arms manufacturer, the Department of Prisons, the Bureau of State Security, the railway police and traffic police.[23] Some restrictions were also placed on sales to the Bantu affairs agency.[24]

As a cable from the U.S. mission in Pretoria soon showed, Pretoria had anticipated the tightening of the embargo. The confidential cable, which the State Department released to the American Friends Service Committee under the Freedom of Information Act, details a secret South African study of the impact of international sanctions. The U.S. embassy in Pretoria reported to the

State Department that the South African government had quietly set up an economic warfare commission to deal with the threat posed by export restrictions, operating under Simon Brand, an adviser to the Prime Minister.

The release of the cable shed light on an area which has been hidden from public view: despite their political bluster and claims of increasing self-sufficiency, the South Africans are highly vulnerable to restrictions on the supply of foreign equipment. It also confirmed that multinational corporations in South Africa are involved in a plan to bail out Pretoria:

> A grave problem would be the supply of spares for existing high technology equipment. SAG [the South African government] has built up a reserve of stocks of more than one year which will act as a cushion, but there is no possibility all replacement parts for imported goods which keep economy going ('even office elevators') can be locally produced.

Lack of access to foreign technology could cripple South Africa, as the cable points out. The incapacitation of a single computer would necessitate "having to find hundreds of bookkeepers who are not available on [the] labor market." The cable stressed the role of large corporations in thwarting sanctions:

> Multinationals, including U.S. subsidiaries, are determined to undercut any sanctions action *and have already made plans to camouflage their opera-*

---

*"Multinationals, including U.S. subsidiaries, are determined to undercut any sanctions action and have already made plans to camouflage their operation through subterfuges arranged with affiliates in other countries."*
— Cable from a U.S. diplomat in Pretoria to the State Department

---

> *tion through subterfuges arranged with affiliates in other countries.* SAG's [the South African government's] stake in the multinationals is very large, not only for obvious economic reasons but *because they exercise a restraining effect on policymakers abroad.* (emphasis added).[25]

U.S. corporate officials began to put their "restraining effect" into practice shortly after the Commerce Department announced the new restrictions. The subsidiaries in South Africa complained bitterly about the controls and lobbied the U.S. Consulate in Johannesburg to have them softened.[26] At first, the subsidiaries were reluctantly prepared to go along with the ban on sales to the police and military, as another cable explained, but they pressed the U.S. government to exclude the Department of Prisons, the Bantu Administration Boards, the secret police, ARMSCOR and other agencies from the embargo.[27] Later, as a letter from the American Chamber of Commerce in South Africa to the Commerce Department shows, the U.S. subsidiaries argued that the entire ban should be scrapped. A Chamber of Commerce official reminded the Commerce

Department that the organization represents 250 U.S. corporations with business interests in South Africa, and claimed that "profits and dividends will suffer" as a result of the embargo.[28] Senior U.S. officials from the home offices of IBM, Motorola,[29] Control Data Corporation[30] and other multinationals registered their opposition to the ban and asked that it be lifted.

### The Arms Embargo—Reagan-Style

It now appears that the corporate effort waged on both fronts to scale back the embargo is beginning to pay off. The Reagan Administration started chipping away at the embargo in the summer of 1981, announcing that South African police and military entities would no longer be prohibited from receiving equipment "used to prevent unlawful interference with international civil aviation." The change reflected the U.S. interest in preventing "international terrorism," according to the government.[31]

The new provision seriously weakened the embargo but it was only a portent of worse things to come. A few months later, the Administration authorized the sale of a Sperry computer to Atlas Aircraft [32] and on March 1, 1982, the Commerce Department issued sweeping new regulations significantly relaxing controls on exports to the police and military.[33] The Commerce regulations continued the ban on sales of weapons but they lifted curbs on several categories of potentially sensitive exports. Among the highlights of the Reagan changes:

- Requests to export aircraft and helicopters to South Africa will be "considered favorably on a case by case basis" provided they cannot be put to military or police use;
- Exports to the police and military of personal computers and communications equipment, anti-hijacking gear and a broad range of products not subject to "national security controls" will generally be allowed as long as they do not contribute significantly to security operations;
- Sales of U.S. components and equipment to Pretoria's security forces from foreign countries will generally be allowed when they are incorporated in a larger system and make up no more than twenty percent of it;
- The re-export or re-sale of "insubstantial portions" of goods or technical data to Pretoria's police or military will be allowed if the commodities would not play a major role in security operations;
- Computers and other products destined for most South African agencies, the Council for Scientific and Industrial Research and the subsidiaries of ARMSCOR will be considered favorably for export unless they would be used to enforce apartheid.

The new controls are hobbled by a lack of precision and specificity, a situation which gives enormous discretion to licensing officials and the multinationals. U.S. exports to the security forces are only supposed to be denied if the product under question is on the Commodity Control List or if it would contribute

# IBM

## Sharing a world of experience to meet South Africa's needs.

In less than a generation, IBM employees in South Africa have increased from four to over 1,400. In less than a generation, IBM customers can be found from Sibasa to Mossel Bay, from Richards Bay to Oranjemund.

This growth has been based on the successful interaction between technology, dedicated staff, and a resulting customer confidence—three sound ingredients for the years to come.

*IBM's 370 computer is used by many South African government agencies. Maryknoll*

"significantly" to military or police operations. Yet, an official at the Office of Export Administration acknowledged that the Commerce Department has no criteria to determine how useful an item might be to the South African security forces. Such criteria, he said, would be "developed on an ad-hoc basis."[34]

What has significant police or military applications? Taken alone, an ink pad is hardly a tool of repression. But in the hands of police officials it can be used to fingerprint Pretoria's opponents. Is microfilm a strategic commodity? Perhaps not intrinsically so, but when used by an ARMSCOR subsidiary it can help scientists retrieve technical data for a weapons project within seconds. Will a microprocessor make a significant contribution to military operations? Even though it may make up only 10 percent of the cost of a piece of hardware, a microprocessor can help aim and deliver a missile to its target. It appears that the new regulations will permit U.S. multinationals to sell seemingly neutral products of this type to the South African military and police. Of course, once the products are under the control of the security forces, both the Commerce Department and the corporations are powerless to prevent them from being used against the majority population.

# CHAPTER THREE

## ADMINISTERING APARTHEID— U.S. COMPUTER SUPPORT FOR THE SOUTH AFRICAN REGIME

DEPARTMENT OF PLURAL AFFAIRS LOG IN. 8/23/81. 4:00 AM. TYPE. GIVE ME THE NAMES AND ADDRESSES OF ALL BLACKS ON VIC- TORIA STREET. INCLUDE PASS NUMBERS AND FINGERPRINTS. DUPLICATE TO HEAD- QUARTERS SOUTH AFRICAN POLICE. TIME: 4:01 AM.

. . . *Preparations for an early morning raid. The target: "Illegal" blacks and political opponents of the regime. With a burst of speed, the computer flashes the requested data on to a screen in front of the operator, while a printer clatters out a paper copy. At the same time, the information is electronically transmitted to the police. . .*

The South African government doesn't disclose many details about its opera- tons, but if it did, this is how the prelude to a sweep through a black township might look. Imported computer technology makes this type of operation simple in South Africa.

In 1977, one year before the U.S. tightened controls on exports to South Africa, the Pretoria regime announced what everyone already knew: South Africa was engaged in a Total War to maintain white minority rule. South Africa's Total War, demanded a "Total Strategy," a prescription for a militarized national security state which has integrated all branches and all levels of the government, the country's industry and businesses, the educational system and other institutions into the struggle to preserve white political control.[1]

"The maintenance of the sovereignty of the Republic of South Africa is the combined responsibility of all government departments," said the regime in its 1977 *Defence White Paper.*[2] South Africa's minority government is highly centralized and tightly controlled, making it easy to marshall different agencies together to defend the country's "sovereignty." Several government agencies, in effect, serve as the front line in the Total War by administering the apartheid system.

The U.S. Commerce Department's ban on sales to certain South African agencies was ostensibly designed to prevent the export of equipment which would be used to support the South African policy of apartheid.[3] Yet the regulations do not affect the sale of sophisticated hardware to a wide range of government agencies that perform strategic work and maintain internal security by monitoring, coercing and conditioning South Africa's majority. This control is shared among several authorities including local and provincial government bodies, transportation and communication officials, the segregated educational system, planning agencies and similar groups.

More than any other single technological advancement, the computer has fostered the concentration of administrative power in the hands of South Africa's white elite. Since the days of the first automated population register, computer use has spread to virtually every government department, playing a key role in Pretoria's ability to manage the African, Asian and Indian population.

### Apartheid's Memory Bank

With headquarters in Pretoria, the Plural Affairs Department, formerly known as the Bantu Affairs Department, plays a key role in the government's regulation of the African population. The Plural Affairs computer network, which is based on British-made ICL hardware, stores fingerprints and personal details on the 16 million South Africans whom the regime classifies as blacks.[4]

---

*More than any other single technological advancement, the computer has fostered the concentration of administrative power in the hands of South Africa's white elite.*

---

Not far from the Plural Affairs Department in Pretoria, at the start of every business day, nearly 100 faithful state employees report for duty to a restricted area of the headquarters of the Department of the Interior that houses the "Division of Data Processing." Access to the Division is off-limits for good reason; it is a sensitive installation which houses the other major part of the apartheid system's registry — a computer base with files on another seven million people who are considered to be non-blacks.[5]

Together, the Plural Relations and Interior Department's data systems make up apartheid's automated memory bank, giving the minority regime a degree of control that is unrivalled throughout Africa.

### Interior Department Computer System

Since at least 1970, the Department of the Interior has relied on IBM hardware for its portion of the computerized population registry.[6] Over the last ten years, new computers and peripheral equipment have been added to expand and up-grade the system's capability. Today, Interior Department operators use two IBM Model 370/158 mainframe computers. Files stored on magnetic tape and disc drives are retrievable by operators working at several terminals. The IBM system processes and stores a vast quantity of details about the seven million South Africans including data such as identity numbers, "racial classification"—white, coloured, Cape Coloured, Malay, Chinese, Indian or Griqua—names, sex, date of birth, residence, photo, marital status, drivers license, dates of departure from and return to the country, and place of work or study.[7] The same IBM computer functions as the basis for the "Book of Life," an internal identity document issued to all South Africans covered by the Interior Department databank. When questioned about IBM's role in the expansion of this system, an IBM official replied, "We feel that the fact that it is being done with computers hasn't any appreciable overall effects on the apartheid situation. This pass system could be done in many other ways besides computers."[8]

In January, 1981, Interior Minister Chris Heunis proposed an expansion of the identification system. Under the new plan, all population groups would have to submit to government fingerprinting, a requirement which currently only applies to people the regime classifies as black. "Fingerprints are the only irrefutable proof of identity;" the compulsory nationwide fingerprint program would help limit "increasing attempts to infiltrate strategic installations and national key positions with a view to espionage and/or sabotage," according to Heunis.[9]

The IBM computer system used by the Department of Interior facilitates the very system of racial classification that undergirds apartheid. It also provides an efficient method of tracking South Africans' movements for security purposes. In the face of all this evidence however, IBM insists that it is politically neutral, and claims that it won't do business where its equipment will be used for repressive purposes.[10]

Since exports to Pretoria's Interior Department are generally allowed by the U.S. government, IBM will likely continue to provide hardware to the Department's Data Processing Division. As the Interior Minister reported in 1978, the Department has been considering establishing new regional data-gathering facilities to back up its central computer installation.[11] New satellite data processing centers of this type would extend the reach of the apartheid memory bank and would likely result in new contracts for IBM.

### Watching the "Bantu" Public

Although the prospect of a new string of Interior Department computer centers, and mass compulsory fingerprinting both signal Pretoria's intention to tighten its grip on Indians, Asians, coloureds, and whites, the black population still endures the greatest degree of government surveillance and repression. Much

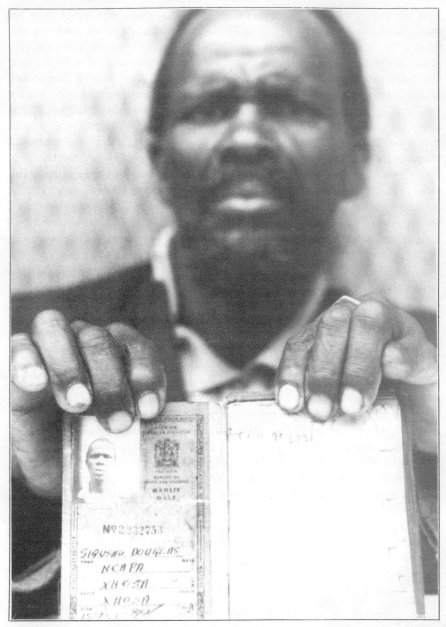

*Computers help streamline Pretoria's national identity system. United Nations/Contact*

of it is inflicted by the Department of Plural Affairs, the agency whose purpose, the government claims, is "to aid with the administration of blacks and guide them in their advancement toward self-determination."[12] One of the Department's main functions is to administer the country's influx control system, a key feature of the Total Strategy. Influx control is the government's method of channeling needed black workers into the labor force and confining other blacks to South Africa's marginal, desolate reserves, known euphemistically as homelands. Influx control would not be possible without the hated passbook, which, if properly endorsed, gives its bearer the right to work or live in "white areas." Improper endorsements or failure to produce a pass can lead to arrest and jail.

The passbook system is based on a sophisticated computerized system which stores identity records and fingerprints from millions of Africans designated as blacks.[13] "The fingerprint record," says the Department, "is absolutely essential because it guarantees positive identification and precludes the possibility of foreign blacks infiltrating into the Republic . . . "[14] All blacks are automatically subjected to fingerprinting at the age of 16. With fingerprints and personal data being fed into the automated system every day, the volume of the Plural Affairs Department's grim operations is staggering. In 1978, the Department had 15 million sets of prints stored in its central computer, and during the same year, the agency issued nearly 900,000 new passbooks and identity documents to South African blacks.[15]

The repressive nature of the Department's computer bank has not gone unnoticed even in South Africa's white business community. One business writer described the system as "Computers flashing out reference numbers, photocopies relayed by telephone, perhaps even instant transmission of fingerprints — all to keep track of members of the population. Sounds like George Orwell's *1984,* doesn't it? Well it's SA's way of modernising and streamlining its pass and influx control system."[16]

The British manufacturer ICL supplied the Plural Affairs computers.[17] Although ICL is based in the United Kingdom, the company has a manufacturing facility in Utica, New York which produces video terminals that could have been supplied to the Plural Affairs Department as part of the system. According to one U.S. computer industry guide, the type of computers ICL sells to the South African government contain "many U.S.-built components and peripherals."[18]

### Plural Affairs Network

Pretoria's Plural Affairs Department operates through a network of fourteen regional Bantu Administration Boards, which, the government says, "will, to an ever increasing extent, become the bodies on which the black laborer will rely for his physical and spiritual welfare while he is employed in white areas."[19] The Boards, which serve as the arm of the minority government in the black townships, are made up of whites only and represent sectors of the economy with an interest in using and controlling the black urban population, such as industry, commercial organizations, the white unions, and local white government agencies.[20] The Bantu Boards run the hostel system that houses many of the black workers who are not allowed to have their families with them. They also collect rent for group housing, run the Bantu tax system, and administer a complicated system of permits and controls which govern the movements of blacks.

Little information about the Boards' computer system is disclosed in South Africa, but the local computer industry press has indicated that the Bantu Boards have at least eight computers – all of them supplied from outside the country. Four of the computers are from ICL; four are furnished by U.S. corporations. Of the U.S. installations, three were apparently put in place before the U.S. began to place some controls on sales to the Department of Plural Affairs in 1978. One was installed in 1980.[21]

The East Cape Administration Board, one of the largest in South Africa, uses a computer configuration based on a Burroughs 711, an ICL unit, plus printers and terminals. Burroughs' South African subsidiary rents this computer to the Board for R1300 per month. The system uses magnet tape and discs, which can locate and retrieve data within seconds.[22]

Like other Bantu Boards, the East Cape Board is responsible for administering a series of repressive laws and directives which regulate the lives of all blacks in the large area under Board control. Police actions against blacks in the area are

---

*Two U.S. computer suppliers have furnished hardware to the East Rand Bantu Administration Board which has jurisdiction over thousands of blacks in a large area to the east of Johannesburg.*

---

common. South Africa's Institute of Race Relations keeps a running account of them: " . . . In January, raids were conducted against squatters in East London's Second Creek and Mpuku Streets. Twenty-one people were arrested, convicted and sentenced to R10 or twenty days imprisonment each . . . In February, East Cape Administration Board officials commenced with the removals and 'repatriation' to the homelands of squatters from these camps. Many squatters were reported as fleeing into the bush to escape removal . . . Raids by board officials were conducted against Parkside (East London) squatters in November . . . The squatter camp at Frankfort (King Williamstown) was demolished in March and the 150 families were resettled in an adjacent area . . . "[23]

Two U.S. computer suppliers furnish hardware to the East Rand Bantu Administration Board, which has jurisdiction over thousands of blacks in a large area to the east of Johannesburg. The Board's computer installation, in place since 1976, is based on a large Burroughs 3700 unit, and a model 1200 minicomputer supplied by Mohawk Data Science.[24] The East Rand Board pays Burroughs and Mohawk R228,000 per year to rent the computers — over a fourth of what it spends on housing for blacks in an average year.[25] These computers are used to register blacks for the labor allocation system, and to administer the Board's financial matters. Although the Bantu Boards are directly involved in the implementation of apartheid, the flow of hardware to them has not stopped. Despite the embargo, the East Rand Bantu Administration Board installed a model 399 unit supplied by NCR some time during 1980.[26] Blacks in the East Rand area are at the mercy of Administration Board police and the national police. Over 70 people are arrested in the area on an average day for pass law violations.[27]

---

### BUREAUCRATIC VICIOUS CIRCLE

"If a person did not have a birth certificate when he applied for his first reference book, his birthplace is frequently incorrectly entered in the application form," according to Sheena Duncan of the Black Sash, who added that blacks are not allowed to fill out their own passbook applications, and are frequently not given the opportunity to check the information before they are ordered to sign. Duncan noted, "Sometimes the father's birthplace or the area in which they are at school are put down as their birthplace and this information is stored with the fingerprints in the computer." Duncan says errors like this can have unbelievably disastrous consequences. If an African living in an urban area wants to establish his "right" to remain in the town where he was born, he must apply to the government for permission and produce a birth certificate. "He therefore applies for late registration of his birth. He is told that his birth cannot be registered until the computer record is corrected. He goes to the office of the Commissioner to make his application with proof of his birth and is told his application cannot be accepted," until he has been "influxed," or given official permission to remain in the area. He then goes to the Administration Board Office to ask to be "influxed and is told this is impossible until he has a birth certificate. . ."

From *The Black Sash National Conference 1980*, Johannesburg Advice Office.

---

### Expanding the Apartheid Memory Bank

In November, 1980, the regime announced that it was considering a plan to expand computer surveillance of blacks by establishing a national network linking the Administration Boards and the police to a central computer in Pretoria. The new system was trumpeted as a measure that would reduce unemployment "by providing instant information on where jobs are and where workers are who can do the jobs." The network, which is under consideration in senior government circles, would amount to a vast national tracking system for the country's blacks, even more comprehensive than the one already in place.

*Waiting to be processed at the pass office.*

Personal details fed into the computer would include educational qualifications, test results, employment histories, criminal records and "ethnic origins" of urban blacks and their status under influx control laws. The press also reported that the computer network would be programmed for "message input" by the police to pinpoint people who are required for questioning.

Apártheid critics denounced the proposal as marking a new era of control which, according to opposition spokeswoman Helen Suzman, "will make the pass system seem like child's play." Activist Sheena Duncan, a leader of the white women's organization called Black Sash, saw the regime's Total Strategy at work behind the plan. "Obviously, now they plan to link up and keep a stricter watch on black people's movements," commented a black leader.[28]

The new computer system would be managed by the Department of Manpower Utilization, an agency authorized by the U.S. Commerce Department to receive U.S. exports on a case-by-case basis. U.S. computer companies in South Africa would presumably be free to bid on this project and supply the new equipment as long as they can make a case that the system would not enforce apartheid.[29]

### Computer Use By Other Central Government Departments

Since computers are regarded as a strategic commodity, and because computer suppliers are subject to growing pressure from shareholders, unions, churches, campus groups and other activists in the United States, the South African government discloses little detailed information about its installations. It is clear, however, from information pieced together from the few accessible sources, that U.S. computer corporations are deeply involved in supplying virtually every branch of the regime.

In addition to its use in the national identity system, U.S. hardware is indispensable to a wide range of operations in several state departments. For example, IBM provides the Department of the Prime Minister with a Model 370 mainframe for data storage and processing. The South African Reserve Bank uses a Univac 1100/12 furnished by Sperry Rand. Escom, South Africa's electrical utility, uses two mainframes supplied by Control Data. Data General has supplied the government with over 85 computers. Mohawk Data Science computers are used in the Treasury Department (See the appendices for a list of computers used by various departments and parastatal agencies).[30]

The Pretoria regime acquires many of its computers through the State Tender Board, a central procurement agency for several departments, including the Directorate of State Auxiliary Services, the military forces, the Department of Plural Relations, the Department of Public Works, the homeland governments, telecommunications and transportation agencies.[31] Many of these agencies are either military-related or perform internal security functions. The homeland administrations, for example, control the black population confined to the reserves. The Post Department helps oversee strategic electronics and telecommunications research. The Department of Public Works builds South Africa's jails, military bases, police stations and other government installations. The Department also installs police communications systems and electronic security devices — all acquired through the State Tender Board.

A six-month survey of the *State Tender Bulletin,* where many government purchases are announced, shows that this supply channel is widely used to procure U.S. computer hardware and electronics. ITT, Rockwell, Hewlett-Packard, 3M, Data General, Perkin-Elmer and Centronics are among the U.S. manufacturers of equipment sold to government agencies through the State Tender Board during the period surveyed.[32]

U.S. law apparently does not restrict sales of high-tech equipment made by U.S. corporations through the State Tender Board, despite the links many of these agencies have with the military, and in spite of their strategic importance. When necessary, the State Tender Board can also be used as a supply conduit for the few South African government agencies that *are* embargoed by the U.S. and other members of the United Nations. By funneling bids and purchasing through a central procurement agency like the Board, the white government can easily conceal the ultimate end-user of any U.S. equipment and thereby circumvent the embargo.

Although it is difficult to trace such sales for obvious reasons, one can speculate how they might occur. For example, a high-speed computer requisitioned

THE DIVISIONAL COUNCIL OF THE CAPE

P.O. Box 1073
Telephone: 41-3266

44 Wale Street,
CAPE TOWN.
8001

DATE: *5/10/77*

Mr./Mrs. *W. Mbonyana*

Structure No. *402*

Dear Sir/Madam,

PROPOSED DEMOLITION IN TERMS OF SECTION 3B OF THE
PREVENTION OF ILLEGAL SQUATTING ACT, 1951 AS
AMENDED.

Please note that within *5 Five* ~~7~~ days of the date hereof my Council
intends to demolish the structure which you are occupying
without legal permission in contravention of Section 1(a) of
the Prevention of Illegal Squatting Act No. 52 of 1951, as
amended and to remove the material thereof from the land.

Yours faithfully, *Cinaphume lelango nemigaye yokansi*
*yokingehlawuli imali efekanshle*
*elu Luvazise lelo Kuggabela*

for W.R. VIVIER
S E C R E T A R Y

I hereby certify I have served a copy of this letter on
*W.R. Angelina Monyani*

Place: *Gilheads*

Date: *6/10/77*

*Monyani*
SIGNATURE

*Eviction notice. National Union of South African Students*

through the State Tender Board, and sold, ostensibly for use by the railway department, could easily be put at the disposal of the miltary. U.S. facsimile transmission equipment, ostensibly destined for the post office could be diverted to the National Intelligence Service and used to beam information and fingerprints from field posts to headquarters. There is little to prevent electronic components, procured through the State Tender Board for a project of the telecommunications agency, from being re-routed to an arms plant for use in battlefield sensors destined for the Namibian-Angolan border.

### Computer Use By Local Government Agencies

While U.S. multinationals have made a substantial contribution to the growth of computer use in a myriad of central government departments, they have also helped computerize South Africa's white-dominated local and regional government bodies. In the '50s and '60s, before the computer boom hit South Africa, few municipalities had computers. Those few used them mainly for simple accounting.

The U.S. government's restrictions on exports to certain agencies did nothing to stop sales to local government bodies. Due in large part to skillful marketing on the part of U.S. corporations, South Africa's white authorities have jumped on the computer bandwagon in large numbers. As a result, U.S. firms are sustaining most of South Africa's larger, and many of the country's mid-sized local governments with computer hardware, programs and service.

*. . . U.S. firms are sustaining most of South Africa's larger and many of the country's mid-sized local governments with computer hardware, programs and service.*

It is impossible to divorce U.S. hardware from the setting in which it is used every day. In many cases, U.S. corporations are supplying computers to the very same agencies that are responsible for the legally-enforced indignities inflicted on blacks, Indians and Asians who live or work in official "white" areas. One incident which occurred in Boksburg demonstrates this fact. There are undoubtedly many others like it. Like all other cities in South Africa, racism is written into local law in Boksburg, a town located in the Transvaal, a province in the northeastern part of the country. The local white administration maintains rigid segregation of virtually all the facilities under its control, according to the *Race Relations Survey*.[33] When students in a nearby area which the the government has classified as coloured applied to use the Boksburg city hall for a fundraising dance, the city council refused them. A city official reportedly told them that "the coloured community needed uplifting before it could be allowed to use the hall." The council also said that since taxes paid by whites financed the building, it should be reserved for whites only.

The fact that the local administration is controlled by white supremacists did not prevent Sperry Univac from selling Boksburg a sophisticated computer-run municipal adminstration system, based on a Univac 9030 processor.[34] Sperry, however, is apparently no more eager to outfit local white-administered agencies than other U.S. computer companies in South Africa. According to one trade reference, IBM furnished a model 3/15 computer to the Pretoria "Peri-Urban Areas Board."[35] IBM computers are also used by white authorities in Germiston, Newcastle, Randfontein and other municipalities. NCR, which has been a strong force behind the drive to computerize local government agencies, has provided hardware to Pietersburg, Stellenbosch, Rustenburg and other cities. NCR has also launched a specialized software package for local use, "designed in South Africa to meet local government requirements."[36]

There has been a rapid increase not only in the number of government computer installations, but also in the applications the hardware is used for. Local agencies in South Africa are now moving toward what Pretoria specialist P.E. Claassen called "total computerization of local government," following the lead of many U.S. cities. The new model is based on an "integrated information system" which consists of a large central computer with remote terminal links for planning agencies, engineers, adminstrators, educators and the police. In addition to concentrating information and power in the hands of white officials, this all-encompassing computer system can be used to monitor the population. As a benefit of the system for security planning, notes Claassen, "Concentrations of

---

*Given what the South African Defence Department calls its "increasingly important role in local government," it is axiomatic that any U.S. computers sold or leased to white civilian agencies are automatically at the disposal of the military.*

---

crime can serve as indicators of problem areas. Changes in the crime rate can serve as an advance warning mechanism."[37] Given the lack of restrictions on the use of computer-stored information in South Africa and the omnipresent national security mentality, local computers will undoubtedly increasingly be used for police purposes.

The Total Strategy has brought with it the militarization of civilian institutions. "The state machinery as a whole is effected," pointed out a South African military journal in 1979.[38] "In order to maintain the greastest degree of readiness, there must be constant cooperation between the South African Defence Force and the central and municipal authorities." Given what the South African Defense Department calls its "increasingly important role in local government," it must be assumed that any U.S. computers sold or leased to white civilian agencies are automatically at the disposal of the miltary. Nonetheless, because the U.S. has not placed any restrictions on the corporations' business with municipalities,

U.S. multinationals continue to sell hardware to virtually any agency that can pay for it.

## City Planning – South African Style

Early in 1980, Control Data Corporation began promoting a new "Urban Planning Package" among government employees in South Africa. The computer-based design system makes use of a graphic display terminal and allows government planners to simulate whole developments electronically during the design phase, for example, adding or removing roads, service areas, industrial sites, mass housing for blacks or white housing. The package was described at length in an article which appeared in a South African civil servants journal.[39]

When Control Data learned that the marketing of this software design system had been reported at an international U.N. seminar on the arms embargo[40] in Geneva, the company asserted that since negotiations for rights to the package had fallen through, it had been withdrawn from South Africa. This has not been independently corroborated.

A similar Control Data software package, called *Perspective*, was also unveiled in the pages of the same journal. *Perspective* makes it possible to simulate the urban environment with tremendous detail, viewing planned structures in three dimensions and automatically adding variables such as automobiles or trees to the screen during design. The design, which is stored in an electronic memory bank, can be retrieved at any time in the planning process for review by government and security officials. "The only limitation to the usage of *Perspective* in planning," says Control Data, "is the imaginative power of the user."[41]

While there is nothing intrinsically sinister about the *Perspective* software design system in general, a program of this type lends itself to abuse in the repressive environment in South Africa. This kind of urban planning program could undoubtedly be of considerable value in South Africa because it enables government planners to design black townships and other areas with security and police access in mind.

Control over the population has been an important consideration in planning the layout of the new townships that warehouse thousands of blacks, according to South African researcher, Gerry Maré. "The previous unplanned tenant (freehold) and squatter areas would have been, and are, extremely difficult to control in that any but foot patrols are impossible in large areas. The 'technology of political control' in South Africa, as evidenced by the Soweto uprising (e.g. 'hippos,' 'sneeze machines,' high-powered rifles, tear gas, etc.) demands a system of straight roads and easy access to all dwellings," according to Maré.[42]

In other countries, urban planning at its best can result in attractive, rationally planned communities, designed for the comfort of all their inhabitants. In South Africa, urban planning follows the government's plan for "separate development" and it usually means comfortable, well-situated neighborhoods for whites, and grim segregated townships for coloureds, Asians, Indians and blacks.[43] As long as apartheid exists, police repression will be built into urban planning.

## Computer Use By Regional Government Agencies

The growth in local government computerization has been paralleled by an increase in computer use by regional government agencies, which do not fall under the embargo. The Natal, Orange Free State, Cape and Transvaal provincial adminstrations use hardware furnished by U.S. firms, including Wang, Mohawk, Sperry, IBM and Burroughs.[44]

# CHAPTER FOUR

## STREAMLINING THE SECURITY APPARATUS—COLLABORATION WITH THE POLICE ESTABLISHMENT

Backing up the army of technocrats and state employees who administer South Africa's government departments and regional and local agencies is a sizeable police establishment with far-reaching powers. Its ranks include the secret police and an active-duty force of 35,500 police agents along with a reserve contingent of 20,000.[1] Also included in the police establishment are 110,000 commandoes, hundreds of traffic and railway police and a burgeoning private security industry.

U.S. contacts with Pretoria's police establishment are long-standing and varied. According to former CIA agent John Stockwell,

> The CIA has traditionally sympathized with South Africa and enjoyed its close liaison with BOSS. The two organizations share a violent antipathy toward communism and in the early sixties the South Africans had facilitated the Agency's development of a mercenary army to suppress the Congo rebellion.

Stockwell added that a "cordial relationship" between the two intelligence agencies has continued.[2]

The South Africans have frequently turned to the United States for police training and technical assistance. For example, early in 1971, an official at the U.S. mission in Pretoria reported that the headquarters of the South African Police had made a request for training materials for "fixed and moving physical surveillance procedures and techniques . . . It would be most helpful if we could come up with useful material," he wrote to Washington.[3] During June and July of 1975, agents from the U.S. Drug Enforcement Agency (DEA) visiting South Africa conducted an intensive course on "the latest investigative methods and techniques" in the war against drugs.[4] The nature and scope of the training give rise to suspicion that the program went beyond the immediate issue of drug use: The course was conducted at the South African Police College for 130 police trainees. Researchers Michael Klare and Cynthia Arnson point out that many of DEA's training programs have wider political implications. DEA's international training, they say, has also included "courses in surveillance, undercover operations, raid planning, interview and interrogation, arrest techniques and the use and development of informants."[5]

Although there are no overt government-to-government police exchanges between the United States and South Africa, quiet contacts have continued, in spite of growing international outrage at the brutality of Pretoria's police. The *New York Times* reported in the fall of 1976 that South African police officials had visited the United States to study riot control methods.[6] Today, South Africa's police establishment maintains contact with police in the United States and around the world through the International Association of Chiefs of Police (IACP), an organization of senior law enforcement offficials from around the world based in Gaithersburg, Maryland. A recently published membership list indicates that fifteen South Africans belong to the Association, which sponsors training programs and distributes information about police technology. In 1981, the U.S. gave two South African police officials visas, enabling them to travel to the U.S. to attend the IACP's convention.[7]

### Foreign Technology for South Africa's Police

Details about the police are closely held, but it appears that South Africa's police have had access to imported hardware for several years. According to a South African ex-intelligence agent, the Department of National Security (which was known as BOSS and now goes by National Intelligence Service) maintains a top-secret computer facility with extensive files on government opponents. Among the agency's prime targets are South Africa's churches. According to a press report, the intelligence service collects and stores information from a number of sources, including mail covers, telephone taps, informants and agents. The computer, said one article, "is the heartbeat of the organization. It provides any information stored within seconds, and often this information is called up for research or reference purposes."[8] Bent on maintaining the strictest secrecy possible, the government has not disclosed the origin of its intelligence agency's hardware. But since South Africa relies exclusively on imports for its large computers, it is almost certain the NIS system came from a foreign supplier. Given Pretoria's ability to conceal the end-user of almost any data processing equipment or other technology procured through the State Tender Board, the NIS computer could very easily have originated from the British company ICL or from Control Data, Burroughs, IBM or any of several other U.S. suppliers.

At least two U.S. firms have been implicated in supplying hardware for use by the South African Police in Pretoria. In 1974, two on-line terminals made by Mohawk Data Science were installed in the Pretoria headquarters as part of the police automated "criminal investigation" system, which used a British-made ICL unit for a central processor.[9] Two years later, the police upgraded their system with a more advanced ICL computer.[10] When the British press disclosed that the new ICL unit would be used by the police to help enforce South Africa's repressive pass laws, trade union members in the United Kingdom pressed the company to withdraw from the "morally repugnant" deal, and warned that the company might lose business from other African nations if the sale went through.[11] Despite stiff protests from Britain's labor movement, members of Parliament and the Anti-Apartheid Movement, ICL delivered the series 2900 computer to the South African police. The controversy was re-kindled in March, 1979, when the *St. Louis Post Dispatch* revealed that Control Data Corporation had manufactured and supplied to ICL equipment for use in the police computer. Control Data, as disclosed in the article, is a close business partner of ICL, which is a major supplier of South African military and police agencies. According to the *Post Dispatch,* Control Data furnished ICL with disc drives for use in the police unit. These critical components are the actual mechanisms which store and retrieve data. Control Data admitted that it sells "hundreds of the disc drives" to ICL but claimed that it could not keep track of how they are used.[12]

*Given ICL's dependency on U.S. suppliers for parts, and the fact that it has a subsidiary and an affiliate in the United States, it is almost certain that ICL computers exported from the United Kingdom to South Africa's military and police contain a great deal of U.S.-origin technology.*

State Department records released to the American Friends Service Committee under the Freedom of Information Act now indicate that the scope of the case is actually much bigger than was originally assumed. The formerly classified documents show that ICL sold not one but nine high-speed computers to the South African police, containing nine 9780 disc storage units sent by Control Data to its U.K. subsidiary, CDC, Ltd. under a blanket export license issued by the U.S. Commerce Department. Once the units arrived in Britain, Control Data's subsidiary re-sold them to ICL, which incorporated them into the main-frames destined for the South African police.[13]

Control Data claims that it notified ICL that U.S. regulations prohibited the use of U.S.-made subunits in equipment intended for the South African police, and insisted that its sales to ICL were in compliance with U.S. law. A Commerce Department representative confirmed early in September 1981, that the company is under investigation. On March 3, 1982, the Commerce Department announced that ICL and its South African subsidiary had been fined $15,000 for re-exporting the U.S. equipment to South Africa's police. The Department's announcement made no mention of Control Data's involvement in the deal.[14] There is every indication that Control Data's collaboration with ICL represents the tip of the iceberg. ICL reportedly relies extensively on many U.S. corporations for components and subassemblies, many of which ICL apparently uses in hardware sold to South Africa. According to one U.S. trade reference, ICL computers contain "many U.S.-built components and peripherals."[15] ICL itself says that all European computer manufacturers rely overwhelmingly on U.S. and Japanese components.[16] The British giant has its own manufacturing facilities in the United States, which make terminals and other equipment. Control Data and ICL are joint owners of Computer Peripherals, a manufacturer based in Minnesota.[17] Given ICL's dependency on U.S. suppliers for parts, and the fact that it has a subsidiary and an affiliate in the United States, it is almost certain that ICL computers exported from the United Kingdom to South Africa's military and police, contain a great deal of U.S.-origin technology.

Pretoria's national police computer system was designed to be flexible. It can be upgraded and expanded at will by adding new programs and peripheral hardware. In the spring of 1980, for example, the police announced that the Criminal Bureau had launched a nationwide computerized suspect tracking system.[18] Using remote terminal links, police operators at regional centers around the country have immediate access to a secret criminal data bank which stores details about anyone on the government's wanted list.[19] Within minutes after police round up suspects in a raid, stop them for questioning, or pick them up for a violation of the pass laws, computer operators can tell the line officer whether the detainees are wanted.

### Tactical Police Communications

In April, 1979, one of South Africa's largest distributors of electronics and communications gear, United Electronics Corporation, unveiled a new mobile communications system, imported from the United States. The system, which is known as TAC, was made by the U.S. communications giant, RCA. An article in the South African journal *Electronics and Instrumentation* promoting the new gear explained that the radio system is designed to provide "communications for *public safety* [i.e. police], industrial and business organizations."[20] Despite its potential police application, RCA received a license from the Commerce Department to export the TAC system to South Africa.

A month after the TAC equipment hit the South African market, the press announced that the police were setting up an advanced new communications network, covering Johannesburg and the entire surrounding area. Its name: TAC, which the press report said, stands for "Total Area Coverage." The system, which "is the same as that of patrolmen in America and Britain," provides an instantaneous link between police and headquarters. The security police had already begun using the TAC system by the time it was announced. The TAC

*Security squad arresting a demonstrator. United Nations/Contact*

network was to be extended to foot patrols, detectives and the "flying squad" within the year, according to the press report, which claimed that the system would "revolutionize the efficiency of crime fighting."[21]

Despite the apparent connections, RCA denied that the TAC system installed for the Johannesburg-area police is the same as its TAC system.[22] The company said that somebody else must have outfitted the police using the TAC name. RCA did acknowledge, however, that several shipments of TAC equipment to South Africa had been made.[23] The company said that it had noted on the export license that U.S. law prohibited re-sale of the TAC equipment to the police or military. But an RCA representative admitted that "it would be impossible to monitor the end-use of our equipment." He added, "If you're asking me, do we ask them to certify to us whether they sell to an embargoed agency, the answer is No."[24]

RCA has since asked United Electronics for written assurance that none of the TAC equipment had been sold to the police.[25] However, RCA's request, apparently flies in the face of South African laws designed to prevent the disclosure of information about sources of strategic products. These measures prohibit any individual or company in South Africa from disclosing any business information to anyone outside the country, without advance permission from the Pretoria regime.[26] The laws were apparently invoked in this instance: RCA's South African distributor refused to cooperate with the company's request, and declined to provide any information about its sales of TAC equipment.[27]

### Police Software

IBM maintains that it will not sell computers to customers who will use them to further repression, but evidence suggests that the company's subsidiary in South Africa has been supplying the apartheid police.[28] According to the *1980 Computer Users Handbook,* an annual overview of the South African computer industry, IBM markets a police software program locally. The handbook lists IBM's "Law Enforcement System" in a series of software packages available from the company's General Systems Division in South Africa.[29]

*The company's inability or unwillingness to explain how the police program found its way into a published list of IBM products available in South Africa does little to dispel public skepticism.*

To get an idea how IBM markets the police system, and how it is used, the American Friends Service Committee asked the company for copies of promotional literature used to sell the package in South Africa. Responding on March 11, 1981, IBM Secretary James Grady indicated that the South African market for the law enforcement package (and others about which information was requested) was small enough that the company had not developed a special brochure to promote it. Grady did not deny that IBM was selling the package. He wrote:

> The IBM-South Africa company doesn't distribute promotional material on those applications. The marketing people use other marketing methods such as direct proposals, including descriptions of successful applications by other customers.[30]

The police software package proved to be an intense embarrassment to IBM. In April, 1981, the American Friends Service Committee disclosed the IBM package in a presentation at a United Nations seminar on the arms embargo, held in London.[31] The following month, IBM's police system was featured in a syndicated column on U.S. computer trade with South Africa by Jack Anderson, that appeared in nearly 900 newspapers.[32]

In response to these disclosures, IBM began to deny that its South African subsidiary had ever marketed the law enforcement system.[33] One company source said that the mere fact that IBM listed the police package didn't mean that it was available. A representative from the company's Armonk, NY head-

*Police computer operator. Servamus*

quarters insisted that IBM-South Africa had not placed the ad in the handbook.[34] But the handbook editors stated in the same issue, "All information was supplied by the companies and vouched for as accurate by them."[35] In the end, IBM said, "All we can say firmly is that we don't know how the ad got into the *Computer Users Handbook.'* [36]

The IBM explanation raises more questions than it answers. IBM did not start to deny that it was marketing the police software package until the company became aware of the possiblility of widespread negative public reaction. The company's inability or unwillingness to explain how the police program found its way into a published list of IBM products available in South Africa does little to dispel public skepticism. If IBM did not supply the information to the publishers of the *Computer Users Handbook,* who vouch for its accuracy, who did? IBM's claim that its police system is not sold in South Africa has not been independently corroborated. In June, of 1981 the U.S. Commerce Department's Office of Export Administration started an investigation of IBM which may bring further details to light.[37]

### High-Tech Equipment for Pretoria's Police Industry

Backing up South Africa's official police force is a private police industry that has gone virtually unnoticed outside the country. It is made up of several companies that supply armed guards, conduct military training courses and sell a range of surveillance and security gear. Although this "hidden" sector of the police establishment has received little public attention, it is making a substantial contribution to Pretoria's Total War.

"A progressive threat urgently requires heightened security measures to maintain the viability of industries involved in military work," according to two senior security consultants. As they noted:

> It is the industrial sector that has the responsibility of supplying the Defence organisations with the material that they need to be able to function in their specific role. So from the military point of view it is essential that the source of supply be secured against all possible threats. The production and manufacturing of components could in most instances have a tactical or strategic influence on our country's military ability. An organisation need not be specifically associated directly with the manufacture of military components. The manufacturing potential and production of an organisation could also have an indirect relationship to defence.[38]

Thus, virtually any industry has implications for the military survival of the country, claim these specialists, adding that South African companies face increased threats of espionage, subversion of employees and sabotage from the country's political enemies.

Most of South Africa's security companies, and many local large industries, belong to the Security Association of South Africa, an organization with 750 members, which says it has "expanded rapidly in an atmosphere of rising tension in South Africa."[39] Says the Association:

> If South Africans, particularly the businessmen of commerce and industry, begin to recognize the danger then they can produce a quiet, efficient army of trained staff ready to deal with the terrorist. A hard nucleous [sic] of people trained to secure their own minds and premises against sabotage, subversion, outside pressures and persuasion, can beat the communist . . . Look around you, and believe that we are the youngest white nation on earth. Look again, and see that we have the best mixed nation on earth.[40]

Security gear from U.S. corporations is apparently widely available locally, although it appears to be marketed more through locally-owned distributors and agents rather than by subsidiaries of U.S. companies. Exceptions to this are Motorola and J. Gerber and Company of New York, both of which have South African subsidiaries that sell two-way radios.[41] Mine Safety Appliances, a Pittsburgh-based corporation, which has sold gas dispensers and masks to the police in Iran and Colombia, also has a Johannesburg subsidiary which markets mining and "general safety products."[42]

A range of sophisticated electronic detection and surveillance equipment from U.S. corporations is available to the private police industry and the government through South African distributors. For example, Westinghouse Security Systems Division offers an "Invisible Fence," to silently pinpoint intruders without triggering alarms by using microwave detectors.[43] Westinghouse also promises "The Ultimate in Security Control" with a system of electronically encoded cards designed to control access to plants and other sensitive facilities.[44]

Another U.S. corporation offers highly advanced electronic sensing equipment which can be used to locate radio signals from a clandestine transmitter – of obvious use to South Africa's private police, the state police and the military.[45] The computer-controlled system, which was advertised in a South African electronics journal, is available from Technology for Communications, International (TCI), a firm located in Mountain View, California. TCI also supplies communications gear to the U.S. Department of Defense.[46]

Norton Company's "perimeter protection system," called Perimalert, was developed in the United States and is available in South Africa through its subsidiary Blane and Company.[47] One of the most sophisticated of its kind, the system was tested by the U.S. Nuclear Regulatory Commission, and according to a South African ad, "is field-proven and industry-accepted throughout the world in nuclear plants, oil companies, chemical plants, utilities, defence installations and prisons."[48] Perimalert is a remotely-operated system that can detect human beings by means of sensors linked to a control center. Norton Company makes the sensors and control units at its Safety Products Division in California.[49] Although the South African distributor promotes the system for use in jails and military facilities, the Commerce Department apparently does not prohibit Norton from exporting this technology to South Africa.

---

*The "Labor Information System. . . provides full information on every worker, from his ethnic group to his merit rating, and also keeps tabs on where every worker is at any one time. . . "*

---

During the Vietnam War, U.S. arms-makers made great strides in applying infrared technology to military surveillance, enabling U.S. troops to "take away the night," as one military analyst observed, by using night vision equipment to detect the enemy.[50] The same technology has since been adapted for use in the security industry and is now available in South Africa. For example, early in 1979, a Johannesburg distributor brought an ultra-sensitive system called Infralarm on the South African market. Made by Barnes Engineering, a Stamford, Connecticut electro-optics company that provided the U.S. military with hardware during the Vietnam War, Infralarm provides automatic interior surveillance of institutional, industrial and military facilities.[51] The system operates silently, and one of its selling points is that it cannot be detected by counter-surveillance electronic equipment. The infrared unit detects people by sensing both body heat and movement. A Barnes representative said the company exports the system through "various U.S. exporting companies."[52]

*Tracking miners with an electronic ID system based on a U.S.-made microprocessor.*

U.S. technology is used not only to keep property under surveillance, but also to keep track of African workers at large installations and mines. A microprocessor made by the U.S. electronics manufacturer, Ontel, functions as the electronic brain of a locally-assembled labor surveillance network, which has been installed in over 25 mines. The "Labor Information System," which reads workers' electronically encoded ID cards, "provides full information on every worker, *from his ethnic group to his merit rating, and also keeps tabs on where every worker is at any one time*," according to the *Financial Mail* (emphasis added).[53] Photo ID systems for monitoring the workplace, manufactured by Polaroid and the U.S. firm Doculum, are also available on the local market.[54] One U.S. firm even helps the South Africans prevent sensitive documents from falling into the wrong hands. Addressograph-Multigraph markets a shredding machine to "turn unwanted confidential paper into safe, illegible shreds."[55]

### Know-How for the Police Industry

In addition to U.S. equipment, Pretoria's private police agencies continue to have access to training techniques and technical information from U.S. business partners. In 1978, for instance, a senior official from the South African company, CBD Training Services, visited a U.S. security firm to work out a deal authorizing CBD to sell security training packages developed in the United States in South

Africa. The terms of the agreement reached with an undisclosed U.S. company allow CBD to provide U.S. security programs adapted for South African security guards and senior security agents. The program covers several areas, including investigation techniques, weapons-use and plans for handling civil disturbances, strikes and espionage.[56]

Two other examples of U.S. training links to the South African security industry involve weapons and lie detector instruction. According to one trade journal, Fidelity Guards, a large South African security agency, sent a company official to Chicago for training at Reid College.[57] Reid, which advertises its courses in a U.S. journal, *The Police Chief,* offers training in the use of lie detector equipment, as well as criminal interrogation and behavioral analysis.[58] Fidelity Guards has since opened up its own lie detector agency in South Africa.[59] Another South African company operates the Armory Academy, a private security weapons and tactical training center, offering "multi-media programs recently developed by progressive law enforcement agencies in the United States."[60]

It is impossible to divorce technology from the context in which it is used. This is especially so in South Africa. Although it is not part of the government, it is abundantly clear where the interests of South Africa's security trade lie. The industry operates in a tight umbilical relationship with Pretoria's police and military. Its mission is to preserve the country's military production base, and keep a tight rein on black workers who are valued for their cheap labor and at the same time feared as a possible source of infiltration and sabotage. Although the U.S. government has placed some controls on the sale of police equipment to South Africa, the restrictions have apparently not been broad enough to cover the equipment described here. Given the mission of the private police industry, its allegiance with Pretoria's police, military and other state departments, and given the complete lack of procedural rights and safeguards for non-whites, it would be naive to assume that U.S. security and surveillance gear sold in South Africa is not used as a tool of repression.

### Police Exports in the Reagan Era

The Reagan Administration's export regulations open the door to direct contact between U.S. multinationals and the South African police.[61] The controls announced March 1, 1982 make it clear that sales of most general products to the police will be allowed as long as they "would not contribute significantly" to security operations. There are many off-the-shelf commodities that may not seem to have potential for police functions at first glance. Yet the regulations are worded vaguely enough to allow the export of several kinds of commodities that may be of considerable value to Pretoria's police, such as computer memories, microfilm and components.

One of the most sinister aspects of the Reagan embargo policy is the go-ahead

*Dog being trained to attack black demonstrators at the police academy in Pretoria. United Nations/Contact*

for sales of "personal communications" (of types "not subject to national security controls") and "personal computers" to the Pretoria police, both to be authorized on a case-by-case basis. The Administration apparently hoped to escape criticism of this loop-hole because of the widespread notion that this type of equipment is not suited to police operations. Personal computers are usually associated with home video games, self-paced learning and balancing the family checkbook. Yet, personal computers — sometimes also called microcomputers — are increasingly being used in police departments across the nation. In the wake of the Administration's decision to lift these curbs, the same trend may develop in South Africa's police departments.

The use of personal computers in smaller law enforcement agencies has been fostered by the Law Enforcement Assistance Agency for several years. One police specialist estimates that between 250 and 1000 police agencies in such places as Elgin, Illinois, Albany, New York, Nashville, Tennessee and Dallas now rely on personal computers for help in crime analysis and other operations.[62] The LEAA, IACP and a few private corporations have teamed up to develop police software specifically for off-the-shelf personal computers such as the Radio Shack TRS-80, the Hewlett-Packard 3000, Apple and Data General machines. Packages designed for personal computers include POSSE (Police Operations Support System) and CASS (Computerized Crime Analysis), billed as a "new weapon" in the "war on crime."[63] Typical applications for small-range computers include the maintenance of master name files, incident files and the "wants and warrants file."[64] "Microcomputers can perform the same criminal justice tasks as large computers, such as providing comprehensive records retrieval . . . ," according to one U.S. company specializing in the field.[65] Microcomputers have also been shown to be effective in surveillance systems and keeping track of prisoners in jails.[66]

The largest producers of personal computers are likely to benefit the most from the regulations allowing sales to the South African police; they include Apple, Radio Shack, Texas Instruments, Hewlett-Packard, Xerox and Data General. IBM recently launched its own personal computer which is expected to be a big seller.

Once personal computers from the U.S. corporations are in the hands of the South African police or under the control of the prison system, the United States will, of course, be powerless to prevent their use to silence Pretoria's opponents. The fact that much of the police software recently designed for microcomputers is in the public domain (and presumably available in South Africa) is likely to make the small systems even more appealing to Pretoria's police.

# CHAPTER FIVE

# ARMING APARTHEID—HIGH-TECH EXPORTS FOR SOUTH AFRICA'S ARMED FORCES AND MILITARY-INDUSTRIAL COMPLEX

*A Little IBM Can Mean a Lot of Freedom*
*—IBM Ad Slogan*

In the spring of 1980, the South African minister of defense revealed the existence of a new naval missile system, which, the government claimed, would rival any in existence.[1] The announcement of the new missile came only a few days after Pretoria disclosed the development of a "revolutionary war ship," and a powerful new 127 mm rocket system. A year later, the new multi-tiered rocket system was rolled out along with other new weapons in a massive display of Pretoria's military muscle at the Republic Day Parade — one of the biggest festivals of militarism in South Africa's history.[2]

The parade gave the apartheid government a chance to show-case its war machine, the most powerful in Africa, and the result of an enormous buildup. Pretoria's increases in military spending demonstrate the government's single-minded devotion to its armed forces. From 1975 to 1980, military spending more than doubled.[3] For fiscal year 1981 alone, the minister of finance disclosed that the government intends to increase arms spending by 40 percent to R2.75 billion.[4] The actual budget devoted to state security is much higher — probably approaching R4 billion — if the cost of the police, judiciary, military construction and related outlays are included.[5]

South Africa is in a state of permanent semi-mobilization, with a total active-duty force of 86,000 soldiers and a force of 260,000 on active reserve.[6] The army is the largest military branch, accounting for 80 percent of its manpower. Soldiers are trained primarily for guerilla war and the army prides itself on its "lightness" and ability to strike quickly. The air force is designed primarily to cover and support ground troops engaged in counter-insurgency operations; the navy is oriented chiefly to coastal defense.[7]

## COMPUTER SUPPORT FOR THE SOUTH AFRICAN DEFENCE FORCE (SADF)

Pretoria's battle to preserve white control in South Africa and Namibia is being fought with foreign-made computers as well as mines and artillery. Automation is no longer a novelty on the battlefield in any country. In South Africa, the computer is especially indispensable because it helps Pretoria fill its critical manpower shortage. The regime draws its forces from a relatively small pool of white draftees, and a potentially untrustworthy group of coloureds, blacks and members of other racial groups. Faced with a widening war for independence in Namibia and increasing unrest at home, Pretoria has mobilized a sizeable military force, and must field as many of its soldiers as possible, rather than assigning them to vital support and backup positions behind the lines. The manpower crunch can be seen most clearly in Pretoria's "tooth-to-tail ratio" (the ratio of frontline combat soldiers to support troops). The SADF is stretched so thin in Namibia for example that it has been estimated that Pretoria has only 1.2 back-up troops (tail) for every one soldier on the front line (tooth).[8]

With every available soldier deployed in the field, computers have become critically important to a range of military operations and support applications, sparing personnel and other resources for front-line duty and increasing overall

---

*It is impossible to keep up with a lean, mobile force unless you use a computer."*
— **South African military computer specialist**

---

efficiency. For example, Pretoria uses computers acquired from foreign suppliers to analyze battlefield data and guide weapons; to transport equipment to the Namibian operational zone — even to send call-up notices out to draftees. According to a SADF computer specialist, "The speed of modern warfare necessitates support and help for several staff officers. It is impossible to keep up with a lean mobile force unless you use a computer."[9]

According to the available published sources, it appears that the SADF has relied heavily on IBM as a supply source. By the time the United States enacted regulations in 1978 to prohibit direct sales of U.S.-origin hardware to the apartheid military, IBM had outfitted the Defence Force with its best computers, including a model 360 unit installed at the Simonstown Naval Installation.[10] A 1974 survey indicated that one model 360 and two 370s were on lease to the SADF.[11] These installations represent only a fraction of the total. According to a confidential source, the SADF has six major computer centers. Following are some of the known applications of U.S. computers and other high-tech equipment for military purposes.

## Directorate for Information Systems and Analysis (DISA)

Using equipment from IBM and know-how from local specialists, the SADF has established a sophisticated military computer network which is housed at the Directorate for Information Systems and Analysis. The DISA network is the military's first computerized command and control system. DISA technicians use IBM equipment for a range of applications and vital operations including research, simulation projects and military software development. A major application of the system, according to the military, is tactical battle planning. Sitting at an IBM video terminal, DISA operators can simulate actual combat conditions that might occur and factor in terrain and geography in order to anticipate problems in a planned military operation before they happen.

The DISA system is pivotal to South Africa's ability to mobilize for war. Its automated personnel data file with details on every member of the SADF enables commanders to hand-pick individuals for special assignments, based on their combat skills or training. Within minutes, DISA operators can provide military leaders with an analysis of every unit in the force, including its current strength, deployment, location, its requirements and problems.[12]

IBM apparently provided DISA with equipment before the embargo was extended in 1978. However, the law now permits IBM to continue servicing this and other facilities as long as the company uses foreign-made parts that contain 20 percent or less U.S.-origin material.

## Project Konvoor

In 1977, the SADF mounted another ambitious new computerization effort, code-named Project Konvoor. Konvoor is managed by a new company, Log-On, which has grown to be one of South Africa's largest software firms. Log-On was set up by IBM staff working on a military project who split off in 1977; the company's R12-million automated military logistics system apparently uses IBM equipment to supply ammunition and military supplies to units throughout the country.[13] Project Konvoor is essential to South Africa's war in Namibia. The apartheid government's Northern Logistics Command in Grootfontein (Namibia) uses the computer network to manage its vital supply channel, insuring "that the men on the border never run out of anything."[14] The system, which enables military operators to keep a constant watch on supply stocks and notify field units when supplies start to run low, is used to requisition and dispatch a range of goods into the operational zone, including communications gear, weapons, armor, helicopters and other supplies. According to the chief of army logistics, Project Konvoor is expected to save the military R50 million per year by streamlining operations. The last phase of the three-year computerization program was slated for completion in the summer of 1980.[15]

IBM insists that it considers Log-On as an embargoed agency, as far as its military contracts are concerned. However, IBM is apparently able to supply the

*Military computer operator at DISA IBM terminal. Paratus 1976*

South African military firm with products Log-On *claims* won't be used in defense work. The full extent of this trade is unknown, but an official at IBM's international headquarters in Armonk, New York, acknowledged that IBM South Africa had sold published technical manuals to Log-On since the 1978 embargo went into effect.[16]

## Computer Control of Transportation

Although the South African Railways (SAR) is not under direct military control, its vital role in the war effort cannot be overlooked. The SAR is responsible for transporting large quantities of equipment — both civilian and military — to and from suppliers and users throughout the country. In order to monitor and manage the flow of cargo and the location of rail cars and locomotives, the SAR established a computerized tracking system based on two IBM processors linked to some 600 terminals at stations across the country.[17] The computer can give the exact load, present location and destination of any freight in South Africa, around the clock. In the case of military transport, for example, the system could respond to an inquiry fed into the computer with, "All cars carrying shells destined for Grootfontein, loaded at Lenz Military Base, now standing at Upington." The SADF's use of the rails is not a matter of convenience. Without the military transport supplied by the SAR, it would be difficult for South Africa to get military supplies and weapons into Namibia. According to *Paratus*, approximately 90 percent of all the military equipment arriving at the SADF's huge logistics support base in Grootfontein, Namibia, come by rail — from 80 to 90 freight cars every month.[18] In addition to the central IBM units, the SAR rail control network employs a Nova minicomputer, made by Data General, and equipment from Westinghouse.[19]

### U.S. Computers for Military Radar

In the fall of 1979, in response to an inquiry from the British Anti-Apartheid Movement, the United Kingdom's Foreign Office confirmed that Plessey, a major British military electronics corporation, was selling radar equipment to the South Africans. In the course of the ensuing controversy, the Foreign Office also admitted that the Plessey radar system included computers made by the Massachusetts-based Digital Equipment Corporation (DEC), and that Plessey was training South African air force personnel on the U.S. hardware.

Radar guidance has been crucial to the air force's pre-emptive strikes against the forces of the Southwest African People's Organization (SWAPO) and it played a key role in the regime's invasion of Angola in the summer of 1981. It appears that the DEC/Plessey radar hardware is destined to become a part of the military's mobile radar system to protect Pretoria's strike forces during deployment.[20]

---

*. . . Pretoria has increasingly resorted to the use of front organizations to procure sensitive equipment for the police and military when this is not possible by other means.*

---

In spite of Washington's policy against collaboration with the South African military, neither the State Department nor DEC have given a definitive explanation of the radar equipment affair. DEC has a manufacturing facility in Galway, Ireland and could have supplied Plessey with the computers from there. In a letter to the Irish Anti-Apartheid Movement, DEC's Irish subsidiary confirmed that a substantial part of the company's business involved sales of its products to third parties, known as Original Equipment Manufacturers (OEMs), who incorporate DEC hardware into their products and re-sell to the end-users. "Plessey is such an OEM," said the letter.[21]

Confidential records released under the Freedom of Information Act to the American Friends Service Committee indicate that the U.S. government was aware of the controversy. In a priority cable dated August 3, 1979, then Secretary of State Vance asked the U.S. embassy in London to provide details and clarification on the Plessey/DEC sale to South Africa.[22] Neither the State Department nor the Commerce Department has provided any explanation for the deal. In April of 1981, Plessey sent a follow-on shipment of air defense equipment from Bournemouth Airport in the United Kingdom to South Africa.[23] Despite repeated requests the U.S. government again refused to supply any details.

## Infoplan

Since the members of the United Nations imposed a mandatory arms embargo on South Africa in 1977, Pretoria has increasingly resorted to the use of front organizations to procure sensitive equipment for the police and military when this is not possible by other means. Infoplan, a Pretoria-based corporation with over 700 staff, reportedly acts as such a go-between for government agencies with military connections.[24] Infoplan is a large and diverse data processing firm offering hardware, software, computer training and services. According to one British specialist, who is familiar with the South African market, Infoplan helps manage the regime's computer stockpile, and the SADF relies on the Pretoria company to provide maintenance and support for military computer installations. Another confidential source says that Infoplan's connections with Pretoria are even more extensive than what has been reported. This source says that Infoplan is actually a creature of the central government masquerading as a corporation. Infoplan reportedly performs a wide range of strategic data processing functions at several sites, including work not only for the military but for the Department of Plural Affairs and ARMSCOR, the state-owned military conglomerate. Several of Infoplan's senior staff are reported to be members of the secret right-wing Broederbond, an Afrikaner organization to which many members of the government belong, reputed to have far-reaching powers.

The British computer company ICL also reportedly has strong links to Infoplan; at least two U.S. companies also do business with the company. Mohawk Data Science rents two series 21 units to Infoplan.[25] IBM, which acknowledges that it is aware of Infoplan's links to the military, has supplied the company not only with parts and services, but also with training and technical data. IBM insists that it does not supply products to Infoplan for military projects, and claims that all its transactions are legal.[26]

## Satellite-Based Communications for Pretoria's Military

The conditions imposed by the United Nation's embargo have made South Africa's quest for military hardware and equipment difficult, but Pretoria is able to overcome many of its supply shortfalls with assistance from U.S. multinationals. Frequently, the government must engage in subterfuge or use clandestine go-betweens to acquire overseas technology. In at least one case, however, a large U.S. corporation has openly promoted an advanced satellite-based communications network with explicity military and police applications inside South Africa.

The network was proposed for South Africa by a General Electric (GE) scientist from the United States in an electronics journal that is little known outside the country. In an article in *Electronics and Instrumentation,* published in the spring of 1979, GE's Dr. Harold Braham explained that the proposed system uses a stationery satellite to link a command center on the ground with personnel using mobile radios. The network has major police, intelligence and military applications. Braham said that ground operators can use the system for

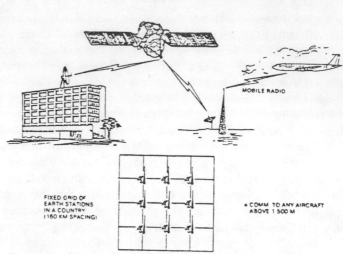

Fig. 4. Nationwide communications to aircraft.

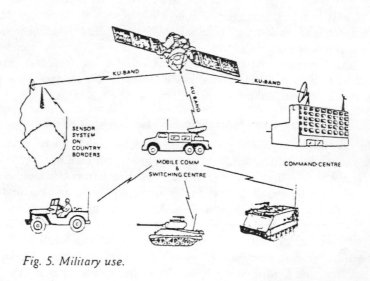

Fig. 5. Military use.

*Applications of a communications system promoted in South Africa by General Electric. Electronics and Instrumentation*

communications with aircraft, and for remote sensing. "Users include not only tanks, jeeps and trucks but even sensors located on a country's borders to observe clandestine foreign intrusion," noted the U.S. scientist.[27]

GE has designed and tested the same type of system for the U.S. Drug Enforcement Administration and the Immigration and Naturalization Service. In a report presented to an international Conference on Crime Countermeasures, held in Kentucky in 1977, two GE researchers described a series of experiments involving satellite-to-ground mobile communications. Their tests included monitoring the movements of an automobile implanted with an electronic transponder as it was driven across the United States; beaming voice and slow-scan television pictures and collecting information from electronic sensors planted along the U.S.-Mexican border.[28]

It takes little imagination to envision the usefulness of this technology to Pretoria's Total War. The police could use it to track the movement of the regime's political opponents. It could provide tactical and long-range communications for military actions in Namibia and incursions into Angola, Mozambique and other neighboring states. It could be used to transmit data from electronic detectors on South Africa's electronic battlefield in Namibia.

The United States has already taken several steps that may make the installation of the GE system feasible. As far back as September of 1960, for example, the National Aeronautics and Space Administration (NASA) announced agreement with South Africa for the establishment of three satellite tracking stations.[29] Two years later the United States installed a military space tracking station, which reverted to Pretoria when the U.S. later withdrew. According to NASA, Pretoria and Washington concluded another Memorandum of Understanding in August 1980, which permits the South Africans to establish a ground station to receive signals from the U.S. civilian satellite, Landsat. The South African Landsat station went into operation in December of the same year. South Africa could modify any of these tracking facilities to serve as a host for the proposed GE network.

The heart of the GE network is the satellite itself. South Africa has no launching facilities of its own and would have to rely on a NASA-launched satellite to serve as the hub of the system. According to Dr. Braham, the South African network could use either of two satellites available from GE: a BSE or a DSCS III (Discus III). The BSE satellite was first developed as a commercial television satellite for Japan. Discus is a series of U.S. government satellites launched by NASA exclusively for military use. The third in this series, Discus III, was launched in the summer of 1981.[30]

The tactical communications system GE proposed for South Africa has disturbing ramifications, and the status of the network remains unclear. The obvious question is: Why was a major U.S. multinational promoting advanced technology of this type among South African electronics specialists over one year after the United States announced a total ban on exports to Pretoria's police and military? It is unlikely that GE would actively promote hardware it wouldn't be allowed to sell. Did the company get a go-ahead from the State Department despite the system's military and police applications? Is the United States sharing access to the military Discus satellite with South Africa?

## Silvermine

In March 1973, the South African military cut the ribbon on a giant new sea-air surveillance and communications center located at Silvermine, near Capetown. The installation, which is hardened to withstand attack with nuclear, chemical, biological and conventional weapons, enables the South Africans to keep a constant close watch on sea traffic in a vast area from North Africa to the South Pole and South America to the Bay of Bengal. The complex is also linked to two regional backup headquarters — one in Durban and the other in Walvis Bay, Namibia.[31] Silvermine was an ambitious undertaking which involved the Armaments Board (ARMSCOR's precursor), the SADF, local contractors and a number of multinationals. Several U.S. communications and electronics corporations were involved in setting up the center, including TRW, Fairchild, RCA, AMP, Inc., Transitron Electronic Corporation and ITT.[32]

The mandatory U.N. arms embargo was not in effect at the time Pretoria established the Silvermine installation, thus the participation of U.S. and other firms in the project was not illegal. Nonetheless, two factors suggest that the United States is still vitally interested and involved in the project despite the arms embargo.

First, Silvermine was built with a tremendous overcapacity which far exceeds any use the South Africans could make of it. One foreign military attaché stationed in South Africa quipped, "It's like having a fully equipped aircraft maintenance facility to take care of a bicycle."[33] This reserve capability could be used for NATO and the United States, both of which are apparently linked to the Silvermine network.[34] Unclassified intelligence from Silvermine is reportedly fed to a U.S. Coast Guard station at Governor's Island, New York. The U.S. naval communications facility at Londonderry, Northern Ireland and a Navy installation in Puerto Rico are also tied to Silvermine.[35]

Second, given the advanced nature of the electronic apparatus installed at Silvermine, it is highly likely that the larger contractors and subcontractors involved in the establishment of the system still provide some support services for Silvermine. Many large military electronics projects include provisions for the follow-on supply of parts, spares, maintenance, testing and training for years — sometimes indefinitely. It is unlikely that Silvermine is any different. Indeed, according to one researcher, ITT supplied Silvermine through STC, its former subsidiary in the United Kingdom. ITT/STC has also reportedly recruited and employed engineers and supervisory personnel for the installation.[36] In any case, transactions through the State Tender Board through Infoplan or through other front agencies would make it possible for U.S. corporations to camouflage their links to the Silvermine complex.

## OUTFITTING SOUTH AFRICA'S MILITARY-INDUSTRIAL COMPLEX

*One South African institute engaged in military electro-optics research uses a Hewlett-Packard computer . . . A state-owned military corporation responsible for providing the military with aircraft uses a Univac . . . Researchers doing work for the military at several institutes have access to a network based on sophisticated IBM and Control Data processors . . . An RCA scientist who has done electronics research under contract to the U.S. military gives a paper at a South African institute that does work for the apartheid military . . .*

Pretoria is indebted to U.S. multinationals for much of its military prowess. The South African government today presides over a flourishing military-industrial complex that has been built and is being expanded with an array of hardware and know-how provided by U.S. high-tech corporations. While the international arms embargo has apparently helped to reduce the direct transfer of arms and large military products to South Africa, it has had little apparent effect on South Africa's ability to manufacture its own weapons. The irony of this situation is self-evident: If it is wrong to sell weapons to the South Africans, isn't it just as wrong — or even worse — to help outfit the regime's arms-makers?

### Structure of the Military-Industrial Complex

South Africa's military industry is made up of a network of production plants, laboratories, testing sites and institutes stretching across the country. The state plays a central and dominant role in the development and production of arms and materiel. Many of these facilities are owned outright by the Pretoria government. Even those that are privately held are subject to government regulation and their work is shrouded in secrecy.

Pretoria's military-industrial complex has three main branches, the first of which is made up of the Armaments Development Production Corporation (ARMSCOR), a company responsible for the development and acquisition of arms, which is owned by the government. ARMSCOR's internal division oversees in-house development in several areas, including ammunition, weaponry, pyrotechnics, aircraft, electro-optics and missile technology.[37] Internal work is carried out by at least nine ARMSCOR subsidiary companies, some of which in turn have their own subsidiaries. One subsidiary, Lyttleton Engineering Works, is responsible for much of South Africa's artillery. Another, Somchem, produces explosives. Atlas Aircraft Corporation, the largest ARMSCOR affiliate, produces South Africa's Mirage jet fighters and other aircraft.[38] An Atlas subsidiary, Telcast, makes aluminum castings for military aerospace use.[39] ARMSCOR's external production division "handles the tasking and procurement control of

*South African troops at the Heidelburg Army training base. United Nations/Contact*

contractors from the private sector in the following disciplines: armored vehicles, operational vehicles, vessels, radar and computers, telecommunications, weapon electronics, maritime technology and electronic warfare."[40]

The second segment of Pretoria's military-industrial complex is made up of several institutes and labs grouped under the Council for Scientific and Industrial Research (CSIR). The Council plays a key role in military research and development (R&D). A government-run organization with several subsidiaries, it provides essential scientific and engineering services and "assists in the defence of the country."[41] Although the CSIR does perform non-strategic work, its involvement in the military sector is substantial and long-standing.

The third segment of South Africa's military-industrial complex consists of contractors — both locally-owned and subsidiaries of foreign-based multinationals — and universities involved in military projects. South Africa spends 65 percent of its military hardware budget on domestic production.[42] According to the government, 100,000 people are employed in private sector military work.[43]

South Africa's military-industrial complex has flourished as the SADF's appetite for weapons has grown. "The growth rate is terrific," noted ARMSCOR Chair, John Maree, who acknowledged that Pretoria's arms industry is now the largest in the entire southern hemisphere.[44] South Africa is self-sufficient in the production of small arms, ammunition (including napalm) as well as jet aircraft, armored vehicles, missiles and naval strike craft.

Though Pretoria has made great strides toward meeting its needs with locally produced weapons as some foreign supplies have begun to dry up, the South African military-industrial complex is still strikingly dependent on imported technology, especially computers, electronic parts and components for weapons. "At the present time, regardless of sanctions, the great majority of all equipment and components required by South Africa are directly imported. For the future, the proportion of local manufacture will certainly increase, but the vast majority of the technology will continue to come from overseas," noted an article about the impact of the embargo.[45] Following is a description of the links between U.S. high-tech companies and South Africa's military-industrial complex.

### Computer Support for ARMSCOR

ARMSCOR had already acquired much of the computer hardware it needed from U.S. corporations by the time the Commerce Department banned direct exports to military and police agencies in 1978. ARMSCOR was on record in 1974 as using a computer rented by NCR.[46] Eloptro, an ARMSCOR subsidiary that designs and manufactures electro-optical systems, uses a 21 MX computer rented from Hewlett-Packard.[47] Sperry supplied a large model 1106 computer to Atlas Aircraft, the subsidiary which manufactures the Mirage and the Impala.[48]

In 1978, the Commerce Department prohibited sales of new U.S.-origin products to ARMSCOR but a loophole in the regulations allowed Hewlett-Packard, NCR, Sperry and other U.S. firms that may have sold equipment to ARMSCOR to continue sales to ARMSCOR *subsidiaries* and to maintain and

---

*"We suddenly found that Sperry-Univac already had the computer there, and we were faced with a* fait accompli.*"*
— **State Department official**

---

supply some spare parts for these installations.[49] The South Africans have been aware of this flaw and it has been touted in the local press. As one South African industry analyst explained in an article entitled "How to Beat a Computer Siege," " . . . it has been established that U.S. companies are allowed to continue servicing existing computer installations on a 'restricted basis' including the supply of parts of non-U.S. origin."[50]

As mentioned, the regulations prohibiting sales to ARMSCOR did not forbid sales to its subsidiaries, all of which have separate names, locations and management structures. The lesser known ARMSCOR affiliates bear innocent-sounding names without any apparent military connections, including "Swartklip Products,"

"Telcast," "Pretoria Metal Pressings," "Kentron" and "Lyttleton Engineering Works."[51]

Exports to ARMSCOR subsidiaries have continued. In October, 1981, the Reagan Administration granted Sperry a license for the export of a Univac 1100 series computer to ARMSCOR's Atlas Aircraft. The Commerce Department licensed the export because Atlas and Sperry claimed that the computer would be used for "inventory maintenance" and would not contribute to South Africa's military potential. The value of a computer, of course, is that it can perform several different tasks simultaneously. Though Atlas indicated that its computer would be used to monitor its inventory, it could easily be used for a wide range of other direct military applications.

There was initial consternation about the Sperry deal in the State Department but Commerce backed the sale. This case illustrates how the multinationals can evade even the nominal control of the "watchdog" agencies that are charged with monitoring the embargo: In the end the government bowed to the company because the transaction had already taken place anyway. "We suddenly found that Sperry-Univac already had the computer there, and we were faced with a *fait accompli*," a State Department official told a reporter. U.S. representatives are supposed to be able to inspect the facility to see how the computer is being used although no schedule for visits has been made.[52]

In cases where exports to ARMSCOR subsidiaries may fall under special scrutiny or restrictions, the companies can simply requisition U.S. hardware through a front company such as Infoplan, through another government agency or through Pretoria's central procurement agency.

### Collaboration with the Council for Scientific and Industrial Research

With a staff of over 4600 working at 16 institutes, the CSIR is the largest research organization in South Africa.[53] Established in 1945, the CSIR is controlled by a council of representatives from the country's scientific and corporate elite who are appointed by the state president. CSIR's annual report emphasizes the agency's "soft" and non-strategic applied research in areas as diverse as fiber science, footwear, air pollution, oceanology and metallurgy.[54] Given the regime's extensive restrictions on information regarding the military, it is not surprising that CSIR's research on lightning or solar energy would receive more public attention than the organization's contributions to South Africa's military potential. Nonetheless, the CSIR is a major part of the military establishment, and together with ARMSCOR, it makes up the backbone of Pretoria's military R&D effort. Its contributions to the South African war effort are reported to include development of the poison gases Tabun, Sarin and Soman;[55] missile research;[56] and work on computerized target acquisition.[57] Two CSIR researchers were awarded police medals "for combatting terrorism" early in 1981 for developing the Casspir series of advanced armored carriers and patrol vehicles.

Since 1972 the CSIR has been developing mobile counter-insurgency vehicles that are praised by the police as "indispensable in operational work."[58]

The CSIR's role in Pretoria's war effort has not discouraged several U.S high-tech companies from collaborating with it, foremost among them Control Data and IBM. This collaboration spans a wide range of activities including the rental of advanced computer hardware and software, training for CSIR staff, visits to CSIR institutes by high-level corporate scientists and subsidies for CSIR programs by U.S. corporations.

CSIR's extensive computer network at the Centre for Computing Services (CCS) is the lifeblood of the entire organization. The presence of a high-level representative of Infoplan on the CCS board indicates the strategic significance of this installation and its work.[59] The CCS facility consists of two large installations based on hardware supplied by IBM and Control Data Corporation. The IBM installation is made up of two model 370/158 computers, several disc drives for storage and instant retrieval of information, and dozens of terminals. A major upgrade in the summer of 1980 more than doubled the capacity of the IBM system. The Control Data installation consists of a large Cyber 174 (currently slated to be upgraded to a powerful Cyber 750 with cryptographic capabilities); seventeen peripheral computer processors and eighty terminals.

The IBM and Control Data equipment, together with various other hardware from other U.S. corporations, puts an awesome amount of computing power at the disposal of CSIR military researchers in several institutes and labs around the country.

The Centre is staffed by 50 computer technicians, but given the overall shortage of data processing specialists in South Africa, the Director recently complained that "it is proving almost impossible to attract white males as operators." In 1980, the Centre was reluctantly considering appointing blacks for the first time. IBM and Control Data provide ongoing training to CCS staff.

IBM and Control Data's collaboration with the CSIR has resulted in a number of collateral benefits for the CCS, including the Centre's access to vital foreign know-how, consultant services and high-level training programs in the United States. U.S. experts and technical advice from overseas are apparently at the disposal of the Centre through IBM and Control Data. For example, in 1978, Control Data brought in a top-flight consultant from its Canadian subsidiary to analyze the CSIR's computer performance and make recommendations for enhancing it. A Control Data lab in the United States also participated in the analysis.[60] A scientist at Bell Laboratories in the United States provided advice on the optimum use of the IBM installation. Senior staff from the CCS also attended technical presentations made by Sperry, Tran Corporation, and others. According to the CCS 1978/79 annual report, CSIR staff attended IBM and Control Data seminars in the United States, as well.

The CSIR's computer center provides access to some twenty CSIR satellite institutes and labs in Johannesburg, Durban, Port Elizabeth, Capetown, Pretoria and Stellenbosch, all of which are linked electronically to the IBM/Control Data facility. Some of these facilities also have their own computers. Many of these CSIR institutes are involved in a range of sensitive weapons-related work. For example, the CSIR's National Institute for Defense Research (NIDR) pioneered in guided missile research and helped develop the Cactus missile.[61] NIDR researchers have recently concentrated on advanced military electronics development.[62] Many of the NIDR's operations have been taken over by another arm of the CSIR, the National Institute for Aeronautics and Systems Technology (NIAST), an agency engaged in the design and development of helicopters and flight systems. NIAST uses sophisticated CAD/CAM (computer-aided design/ computer aided manufacturing) technology in its work.[63] In addition to their access to the central computer facility at CSIR headquarters, NIAST researchers also use hardware from the U.S. company Perkin-Elmer. Among the other branches of the CSIR performing military-related work are the National Research Institute for Mathematical Sciences, the National Institute for Telecommunications Research, and the National Electrical Engineering Research Institute. See the appendices for a more detailed survey of CSIR's involvement in South Africa's military establishment.

## Collaboration With Military Contractors

Most of South Africa's military hardware budget is devoted to the local production of arms and equipment, a trend which has been accelerated by the international arms embargo. Non-governmental contractors make up the third sector of South Africa's military-industrial complex. In this category fall locally-owned corporations, South African subsidiaries of multinational companies, and universities involved in military work. The South African regime parcels out military R&D and production contracts to 800 main contractors and subcontractors.[64] Half of them depend significantly on military work for their existence.[65]

The Pretoria regime is keenly aware that U.S. corporations doing business in South Africa are subject to public pressure at home. Thus, very little information is published about the extent of the multinationals' involvement in private-sector war production. The available information indicates that U.S. high-tech companies are at least as deeply involved with private sector military producers as they are with government agencies engaged in arms R&D.

The South African military-industrial complex is well positioned to conceal the flow of U.S. electronics, computers and communications gear to South Africa, and the use of this equipment in weapons systems and other items intended for military use. For example, military-specification electronics components are easily submerged in wholesale transactions involving hundreds of different kinds of parts. Many of the hundreds of South African companies that produce arms also make non-military products. Thus, a computer for production control, sold ostensibly to help make mining equipment can be used to help forge shell casings for the apartheid military. U.S. corporations, such as IBM, have conceded that it is impossible to control how their products are used, once they are turned over to the end-user.[66]

### Computer Use by South African Arms-Makers

The mandatory United Nations embargo passed in 1977 and the United States' own export controls prohibit the sale of "equipment and supplies used in the production of arms and related material."[67] Nonetheless, several examples indicate that U.S. computers and other equipment are available to, and widely used among, South African military contractors.

For example, IBM rents no less than seven computers to Leyland-South Africa, a firm that produces Land Rovers for the security forces. The police also used locally-made Leyland vehicles in the attack on Soweto and in other operations.[68]

---

*Sandock-Austral, a corporation which has made strikecraft and armored vehicles for the South African military, uses a Burroughs model 1726 unit and a 1955 dual processor. . .*

---

Marconi-South Africa, a military electronics producer (and subsidiary of Barlows, another military electronics giant) uses an NCR 82/70. Two Barlows branches use Burroughs computers, according to trade references. Barlows Electronics Systems division uses a Hewlett-Packard 3000 unit. The Barlow Lab at the University of Pretoria has a Data General Eclipse computer.[69]

Sandock-Austral, a corporation which has made strikecraft and armored vehicles for the South African military, uses a Burroughs model 1726 unit and a 1955 dual processor, according to a recent trade directory.[70]

IBM rents several computers to one of Pretoria's top explosives manufacturers, the African Explosives and Chemical Industries, Ltd. (AECI). The AECI is said to maintain the two largest explosives factories in the world and to manage two munitions plants in the Transvaal for the South African regime. In addition to production of commercial explosives for the mining industry and ordnance, AECI has reportedly specialized in the manufacture of riot control gas, napalm and nerve gas. The company reportedly made the tear gas used against demonstrators at Soweto at its Modderfontein facility which has an IBM computer.[71] A total of four AECI installations use IBM hardware.[72]

South Africa's universities also play a role in the Total War and many of them use U.S.-supplied computers. The universities contribute to the war effort by providing trained conscripts and R&D for the weapons industry. Four of South

*ARMSCOR subsidiaries have access to U.S. technology. This ARMSCOR ad says, "The biggest advances in technology have always been made in the weapons industry — usually during times of conflict." Paratus*

Africa's universities have standing military units — at one of them, the white-only Potchefstroom University for Christian Higher Education, over 35 percent of the student body is in uniform. The Potchefstroom University is linked to one of the CSIR data bases; in addition it has its own IBM 370 plus hardware from Data General. This technology is presumably at the disposal of the University's Bureau of Military Liaison which has conducted some 120 military research projects. According to the SADF, there isn't a department at the university that hasn't been involved in some aspect of military work.[73]

Similarly, the Pretoria Technikon, a civilian institution which is known to train police computer operators and explosives technicians for the SADF's Ammunitions Corps, uses hardware and software from Data General as well as hardware made by IBM.[74]

### Electronics Supplies for Military Producers

The electronic age has revolutionized modern weaponry by tremendously enhancing its accuracy and lethality, making arms highly complex and dependent on a vast number of electronic parts. Today's advanced weapon, according to arms expert, Ulrich Albrecht, is embedded in a weapons *system*, consisting of a large number of different parts which are vital for locating targets, coordinating approaches, aiming the weapon, firing it, controlling it during delivery and reporting on the impact.[75]

---

*Ads for U.S. military electronics in South African electronics journals indicate that access to these products is not a problem.*

---

It is evident that large quantities of U.S. electronic components, sub-assemblies and related technology for military systems are available to South African weapons manufacturers, regardless of the arms embargo. Many of these items have been specifically approved by the Pentagon for use in U.S. military electronic systems. The Department of Defense requires military components to be highly reliable and accurate. Approval for use by U.S. military contractors occurs only after an item is tested by military technicians and given an official military specification (mil-spec) code, or when the Defense Electronics Supply Center in Dayton, Ohio, lists the item on its Qualified Products List (QPL).

Ads for U.S. military electronics in South African electronics journals indicate that access to these products is not a problem. For example, in October, 1978, a South African distributor announced a "new series of miniature bandpass filters for use in aerospace, military and similar applications ... " The series, which "complies with all applicable military specifications," is made by Telonic/ Berkeley, a firm in Laguna Beach, California.[76] An ad in the same journal promotes Aertech coaxial detectors, for use in "broadband electronic warfare system applications," which are manufactured by a subsidiary of TRW, a U.S. electronics conglomerate that is among the top 100 Pentagon contractors.[77]

Germanium Power Devices, an Andover, Massachusetts corporation, markets mil-spec devices, "commonly used as small-signal amplifiers in military computers and military communications equipment."[78] Another South African distributor advertised "Industrial and Military-Style D Connectors" made by Positronics, a U.S.-based manufacturer.[79]

In addition to individual components of the kind described here, sophisticated U.S. microprocessors are also available on the South African electronics market. An article in a local military magazine reported in 1977 on a new microprocessor-based military repair system, built by Hughes Aircraft Company of the United States. This transportable unit, called the "Technicians Maintenance Information System," based on a Motorola 6800 microprocessor, can automatically pinpoint a failure in a complex weapons system, and tell a technician how to fix it. The Hughes system is apparently available in South Africa, and a local company, Messina Electronics, has started to manufacture a microcomputer it calls *Commander*, using the Motorola 6800 microprocessor. ". . .The Commander has arrived on the scene at a time when overseas computer companies are under pressure not to supply specialised computers to this country, and in particular, to our military forces," according to the military journal.[80]

Another South African journal recently announced the availability of a precision measuring device manufactured by Kistler Instrument Corporation, a division of the U.S.-based Sundstrand Corporation which has supplied high-tech equipment to the Pentagon. Kistler's South African subsidiary markets a high-pressure transducer which the company says is used for "measuring ballistic gas pressure on small arms, guns and detonation chambers up to the highest pressures encountered."[81]

---

*. . . U.S. officials apparently turn a blind eye to Philips military electronics exports to South Africa.*

---

### Philips' U.S.-Made Military Electronics for South Africa

The Dutch-owned company, Philips is known wide and far for its consumer products, which can be found on store shelves in dozens of countries around the globe. In addition to its consumer orientation, Philips has also grown to be a trusted supplier of military electronics gear to several nations, including South Africa. At least five Philips subsidiaries in the United States manufacture military goods: Signetics (with plants in Sunnyvale, California and Orem, Utah); Amperex Electronics (Hicksville, New York); Philips Electro-optics Division (Slatersville, Alabama) and the Magnavox Government and Industrial Equipment Company (Fort Wayne, Indiana).[82]

In the fall of 1980, the Dutch Anti-Apartheid Movement published a study which revealed that military products from Philips' U.S. subsidiaries are available on the South African market, despite the international arms embargo. A notice in a local electronics journal in 1979 indicated, for example, that Philips is marketing its Pyro-Electric Vidicon in South Africa. This infrared imaging assembly, which is used in military night vision equipment, is made by Philips' U.S. Electro-optics Division.[83] The same year the infrared detector came on the South African market, Philips also displayed it at the Military Electronic Defense Equipment Exhibition, held in West Germany, according to Dutch researcher, Sami Faltas.

The Anti-Apartheid Movement in Holland also discovered that military-specification semiconductor memories, made by Philips' U.S. subsidiary, Signetics, are available on the South African market, as is a wide selection of other Signetics and Amperex components. Although the Commerce Department's export regulations apply to all U.S.-*origin* products, even if they are made by foreign-owned companies, U.S. officials apparently turn a blind eye to Philips' military electronics exports to South Africa.

### The Altech-ITT Partnership

A stunning achievement of South Africa's military-industrial complex, one that stands out as a mockery of the international arms embargo, is the partnership between South Africa's major military electronics conglomerate, Altech, and the U.S.-owned multinational, ITT.

Until 1977, ITT was the owner of an advanced electronics company in South Africa. In 1977, a locally owned corporation, Altech, bought the ITT subsidiary, but ITT insisted on maintaining a sizeable holding in the company and did so for three years.[84] The arrangement was brilliant: It gave the South Africans a majority holding in a strategically important company. It allowed ITT to maintain a large stake in South Africa, while reducing its visibility and susceptibility to criticism in the United States. As one South African expert summarized, "It suits ITT to state publicly in the U.S. that it has reduced its involvement in South Africa, but in fact it has never disinvested here. Merely it has relinquished control, and thus its degree of visible exposure, while retaining its financial interest as a substantial minority holding in Altech."[85] As the most dramatic part of the negotiations, Altech secured a licensing agreement that gives it "access to all design, manufacture and technological developments made by ITT anywhere in the world."[86]

It is not difficult to understand why Altech pressed for such an arrangement. In 1980 alone, ITT did nearly $350 million worth of electronics and communications business with the U.S. Defense Department.[87] ITT involvement in Pentagon projects spans several sectors of the defense industry, including advanced strategic communications, radar, tactical communications, electro-optics and electronic warfare, to name just a few. The ITT-Altech partnership had profound implications for the U.S. arms embargo. The licensing agreement between the two companies as reported in the press gave Altech potential access to vast amounts of R&D information, know-how and technology that ITT has built up as a result of its U.S. military work. A cursory overview of some of ITT's recent business with the Pentagon, turns up several production, R&D and management and support contracts of potential use to Altech and the South African military. Among them: the supply of night vision goggles and image intensifiers to the U.S. Army;[88] R&D of missile components;[89] the supply of shipborne radar;[90] work on a classified electronics project at Fort Meade;[91] the supply of electronic countermeasures equipment;[92] and the advanced development of search and track functions, using infrared sensors.[93]

Details of collaboration between ITT and Altech are limited to occasional references in the South African press, but there are indications that Altech has taken advantage of its access to ITT know-how and other contacts with the U.S. giant. In 1978, for instance, a local journal reported that Altech was manufacturing devices to relay electronic signals called data modems in South Africa under license from ITT.[94] ITT's British subsidiary is also helping Altech develop its own high-frequency crystal filters, using synthetic quartz.[95] These filters are vital components in advanced communication equipment.

In 1980, ITT sold the rest of its shares in Altech but the company will presumably maintain many of its business links with the South African electronics giant.[96]

Altech, praised locally as a "South African controlled company aware of its patriotic obligations," also has links with other U.S. high-tech corporations many of which also supply the U.S. military.[97] RCA, Fairchild, Intel, Westinghouse, General Instruments and Motorola all distribute electronic components in South Africa through Altech, thereby giving Altech effective control over vast stocks of U.S. strategic technology, and the ability to funnel it to South African military producers with impunity.[98] Altech, of course, is keenly aware of what its control over large stocks of U.S. electronics supplies means: "By the very wide spread of agencies held by the Altech group, no one company is particularly vulnerable should certain of its supply routes be cut off," said Altech chief, William Ventner.[99]

# CHAPTER SIX

# WHY THE EMBARGO
# ISN'T WORKING

*"You can't read an embargo document through a gold coin . . ."*
*—South African saying*

It is clear that support from U.S. high-tech companies helps bolster the South African state and the war machine that undergirds it. This collaboration gives the white minority the tools it needs to run the government and monitor the population. It makes it easier to move troops and supplies to the operational zone in Namibia, and, as the world witnessed in the summer of 1981, to mount an invasion of neighboring Angola. It gives Pretoria access to technology used for systems to track, target and kill its enemies. It puts advanced equipment at the disposal of researchers working on inventions of death, and it emboldens the apartheid regime to try to beat the international arms embargo.

Why isn't the U.S. embargo against South Africa working? Was it designed to work in the first place? Any assessment of the U.S. government's restrictions on trade with Pretoria has to address two questions:

## What does the embargo overlook?

The embargo was ostensibly placed in effect to further the U.S. government's human rights policy by prohibiting the export of any products that would be used to support apartheid.[1] The export restrictions are as significant for what they *exclude*, as for what they specifically cover. Among the most illogical flaws in the controls are the Reagan Administration's relaxation of curbs on sales to the police and military; the exemption of the National Institute for Defence Research and other CSIR agencies from the embargo and the U.S. government's failure to designate ARMSCOR subsidiaries as off-limits. An embargo which purports to deny South Africa access to weapons and military and police technology by prohibiting sales to a few specific government agencies, but *fails to ban exports to major military R&D and production facilities contradicts itself.*

In addition to omitting state-owned weapons companies from the ban, the embargo leaves room for extensive sales to South African military contractors.

Furthermore, the ban does not even cover several agencies that are deeply and directly involved in the enforcement of apartheid, including the Department of the Interior, which uses U.S. computers to monitor the border and operate part of the national identity system; the Department of Manpower Utilization which would administer the proposed nationwide computerized black labor system; other state departments, dozens of regional and municipal government bodies; and the private police industry.

### Has the embargo made a difference?

An embargo that "really mattered" would eventually have a palpable impact on the apartheid system itself. It would effect the South Africans' ability to operate the minority government, outfit their police and equip their army. There is little evidence to show that the embargo has stopped the supply of sophisticated technology from the United States to Pretoria's security forces and other agents of repression. To the contrary, U.S. export controls have left enough of South Africa's supply conduits intact so as to insure that the Pretoria regime will have continued access to computers, communications gear, electronics and security equipment.

For some time after the U.S. embargo was expanded in 1978, it seemed as if the new measures might really have a long-term effect on South Africa's apparatus of repression and military viability. "1978 will be remembered in South African electronics and instrumentation circles as the year of the American arms

---

*. . . the embargo is at best an occasional mild irritant to the South Africans. More than anything, it appears to be largely irrelevant to the flow of technology from U.S. suppliers to South African end-users.*

---

embargo," wrote a local analyst.[2] Some computer and electronics specialists predicted that the embargo might be expanded, cutting the South Africans off from even more sources of supply.[3] In spite of dire predictions that South Africa might be denied access to U.S. technology, by the summer of 1979 the embargo had begun to lose its sting in the local electronics industry, and the South Africans were quietly taking advantage of the embargo's weaknesses. "South Africa On Upswing Despite Embargoes," came the triumphant claim of the computer industry.[4] By 1981, the embargo's squeeze on the local market was even less an issue, according to a trade source.[5]

As concerns access to most U.S. computers, electronics and much of the U.S. security gear, the Commerce Department's embargo is at best an occasional mild irritant to the South Africans. More than anything, it appears to be largely irrelevant to the flow of technology between U.S. suppliers and South African end-users. The U.S. government's policy on high-tech exports to Pretoria is studded with contradictions, loopholes and blindspots; the major ones are described here:

**Computer Timesharing**: Data processing technology by its very nature lends itself to abuses of the embargo. Hardware sold to one agency can provide computing power to users at several terminals. With teleprocessing networks of the type available from Tran Corporation (a supplier of U.S. police departments), which now has a manufacturing facility in South Africa, and other U.S. corporations, computer access can be spread among remote users in hundreds of locations throughout the country. For example, the computer made by Data General which is installed at the Egg Administration Council in Pretoria could be used by the police or military researchers, working at remote sites.[6] It is known that the Department of Indian Affairs uses computers located at the Natal Provincial Administration by means of a remote hook-up.[7] Regardless of the circumstances under which it was acquired, any computer in the hands of the government is fair game for police or military agencies. According to one local specialist, "There is a lot of underutilized capacity in government computer installations, and *there is no way the U.S. authorities will be able to prevent this capacity from being shared by the defence and police departments"* (emphasis added).[8]

**Overseas Production By U.S. Corporations**: One of the most serious flaws of the U.S. export restrictions is that they apply only to products or technical information of U.S. *origin*. Multinational corporations have globalized their production to such an extent that it is easy to manipulate supply sources to avoid the scrutiny and control of any one national government. All of the larger computer corporations have subsidiaries in many countries, several of which have governments that would be reluctant to restrict sales to South Africa. Burroughs, for example, has operations in forty-nine countries, including subsidiaries in Argentina, Brazil and Chile.[9] Control Data has a total of twenty-six foreign subsidiaries. Its affiliate in Israel, Elbit, which makes computers and military electronics systems, also has a subsidiary in South Africa.[10] IBM has subsidiaries in dozens of countries. The company's system 370 computers, widely used in South Africa, are made in Brazil.[11] Nearly all the equipment sold by IBM outside of the United States is supplied from Europe.[12]

Similarly, a subsidiary in Europe of the Santa Clara-based National Semiconductor Corporation is apparently hoping to sidestep U.S. restrictions and make substantial inroads into the South African computer market by selling large computers made in Japan. Even though National Semiconductor is a U.S.-owned company, its exports from Japan will presumably be exempt from U.S. regulations and the company's distributor in South Africa will apparently be free to sell to the police and military.[13]

The sheer magnitude of sales to South Africa from U.S.-owned facilities outside the territorial United States further underscores the importance of this loophole. According to a South African computer specialist, *over 70 percent of the computer equipment sold by U.S. multinationals in South Africa is manu-*

*Control Data placed this ad for Plato in a South African military journal. Caption says,
"Computer Career? Meet the Instructor who will treat you like an individual." Paratus 1981*

*factured outside the United States.*[14] The terms of the embargo allow U.S. corporations to sell this equipment to the police and military as long as it contains less than 20 percent U.S.-origin parts. The confidential cable on the impact of sanctions against South Africa, described earlier, makes it clear that U.S. multinationals have already made plans to use their overseas subsidiaries to supply Pretoria.[15] IBM has acknowledged that it has supplied non-U.S.-made parts to some embargoed South African agencies that are not permitted to receive equipment from the United States. IBM justifies these transactions by arguing that U.S. law does not restrict them.[16] Another cable from the U.S. mission in Pretoria to the State Department, which was released under the Freedom of Information Act, makes it clear that the government is fully aware of the fact that U.S. multinationals are using this loophole to circumvent the goal of the arms embargo: "It is our understanding that most U.S. firms have been able to continue sales by shifting to non-U.S. sources for components," cabled an official to the State Department.[17]

**Diversion and the Use of Front Organizations:** Export regulations forbid the sale of U.S. goods to South Africa only when the exporter "knows or has reason to know" that the items will be used by an embargoed agency.[18] In most cases the exporter is not required to verify the actual application of the equipment; the regulations stipulate that a "destination control statement" be added to the export license, requiring the consignee to "certify" that the equipment will not be made available to embargoed agencies.

These controls are not sufficient to prevent the diversion of most equipment to the security forces, ARMSCOR, or any other proscribed agencies. The case of Infoplan brings this problem into sharp focus. Although Infoplan does computer work for the SADF, in which IBM agrees it cannot participate, IBM does supply Infoplan with "parts, services, education and technical data which are not embargoed by the U.S. export regulations."[19] There is little to prevent Infoplan from using IBM's products and technical information in military work. The growing use of "third-party" supply and maintenance companies by embargoed agencies in South Africa, makes it difficult to trace the flow of U.S. parts, thereby thwarting the embargo.

The use of the State Tender Board to procure equipment has already been mentioned. In addition, evidence suggests that the CSIR and its subsidiaries are used as fronts for agencies that are embargoed. In 1980, for example, the National Physical Research Laboratory (NPRL) helped the South African Air Force outfit a new spectrometry laboratory with analytical instruments from overseas. NPRL staff visited the foreign supplier on behalf of the military to inspect and test the equipment before it was shipped to South Africa. If South African Air Force officials had gone overseas to purchase the instruments, the deal could very well have been jeopardized. The same year, another NPRL official attended an overseas seminar "on behalf of a sponsor" (probably the SADF); and visited Varian-

MAT, a West German subsidiary of Sperry.[20]

**Training**: Like many other transactions involving high-tech equipment, the supply of computers creates a need for trained operators and support personnel. The U.S. embargo apparently fails to cover training offered in South Africa by U.S. computer corporations, despite the likelihood that these programs are open to government staff, including the military and police.

IBM operates a data processing education center in Johannesburg and runs courses in Capetown, Pretoria, Durban and Fort Elizabeth.[21] The company offers a range of training opportunities, from courses for operators to executive seminars. Subject areas include: systems analysis and design, recruitment, software development, teleprocessing and telecommunications. As mentioned, IBM has also provided Infoplan with training; the company also conducts ongoing training programs for the computer staff at the CSIR.

Like IBM, Control Data has established a training institute in South Africa which offers courses on programming, computer technology and basic electronics, among other things. Control Data's pride and joy is an individualized multi-purpose computer learning program called Plato, a system with civilian, military and police applications. Although Control Data emphasizes the civilian uses of Plato in its advertising, the system is used in the United States for military and police training programs. For example, U.S. Air Force combat crews for the KC10A aircraft are trained with Control Data's Plato system. An article in a U.S. police journal entitled "Plato Teaches Cops," detailed how the system can be used for law enforcement instruction.[22]

The Minneapolis-based corporation is evidently eager to recruit trainees from the ranks of the South African military. In May 1981, Control Data placed an advertisement in the armed forces journal *Paratus*, offering soldiers a "learn-now-pay-later" computer course with a certificate in less than four months.[23] "We have found a job for every one of our successful graduates," Control Data boasted.[24] In addition to its own training facility, Control Data also provides traing for CSIR personnel.

The embargo has had little apparent effect on the availability of technical training to South Africans *in* the United States. The U.S. government has apparently even turned a blind eye to the training of South African police. In 1980, a South African police journal reported that a senior police official had visited the United States for a training program. According to the article, Major Hennie Reyneke, Chief of Technical Education for the South African Police, participated in a course on electronic communications at an undisclosed site in the United States. Reyneke returned to South Africa to establish an elite communications training center for the police.[25]

**Transfer of Know-How**: One of the least regulated loopholes in the U.S. embargo is the supply of technological *information* and know-how through a variety of channels. These include informal contacts between U.S. corporate researchers and their South African counterparts; work performed by U.S. corporations under contract to South African agencies and companies; visits to the United States by South African corporate representatives, ARMSCOR executives and CSIR personnel; the sale of software and license rights for production; and access to corporate computer-based international information networks.

Although the U.S. government considers unpublished technical data as a commodity which must be licensed if it is to be exported, the available evidence suggests that few restrictions are actually placed on the flow of strategically useful information to South Africa.

The flow of know-how between subsidiaries of the same multinational located in different countries is especially difficult to control. Philips, which has been previously mentioned, supplies a range of equipment to Pretoria's military, also gives its South African plants access to R&D from its subsidiaries in the United States, which are engaged in military production. The manager of a South African Philips subsidiary, which distributes components from U.S. subsidiaries locally, made it clear that information on the application of electronic components is available "from our overseas suppliers and is originated in the very highly developed Philips/Mullard/Amperex/Signetics research laboratories."[26] Both Amperex and Signetics are located in the United States, and both manufacture military products.

As cited earlier, the agreement between ITT and its former South African affiliate, Altech, gave Altech potential access to a vast amount of expertise and know-how from ITT's facilities in the United States and around the world.

The use of satellite-conveyed computer links between countries, which is difficult for governments to monitor or regulate, has also been suggested as a way of skirting the embargo.[27] IBM has already facilitated a satellite hookup which links the South African government's merchant marine organization with IBM technical support centers in Britain and the United States.[28] Similarly, Control Data has a worldwide computer-based software access system, called Cybernet, which allows South African customers to tap into and use a wide range of programs from outside the country, in fields such as computer-aided design, scientific research, engineering, industrial production and ship-building, many of which may have significant military applications.[29]

**Discretion in Licensing Procedures:** On August 19, 1981, a federal grand jury handed down a sixty-count indictment, charging four people with selling U.S. computer and communications equipment to the Soviet Union through a West German go-between.[30] The indictment was the culmination of a rigorous 18-month investigation by authorities. The seriousness the U.S. government ascribes to this case stands in sharp contrast to the attention given to high-tech exports of the same kind to South Africa. The discrepancy between the two highlights a serious flaw in the way the United States implements the embargo against South Africa.

Simply put, the United States uses a double standard to evaluate exports to the Soviet Union and South Africa. Many of the high-tech exports from U.S. corporations to South Africa involve "dual-use" equipment with military and civilian applications which the Commerce and State Departments prohibit from being sent to the Soviet Union.

Commodities which are either totally off-limits for export to the Soviet Union and Eastern Europe, or which require special scrutiny because of their potential for use in military systems, are listed in a set of restrictions, the Commodity Control List (CCL), or CoCom List.[31] The CoCom List provides an objective basis for determining whether any given commodity is sophisticated, efficient, or powerful enough to be used in a military system, or applied in another sensitive or strategic context.

A survey of CoCom entries indicates that there are extensive controls on sales of commodities on the list to the Soviet Union. However, there are relatively few restrictions on exports of CoCom-listed products to the South African government, and virtually no restrictions on exports to private end-users in South Africa.

*At least three pieces of legislation — the South African National Supplies Procurement Act, the Defence Act and the South African Official Secrets Act — permit Pretoria to seize equipment it needs in an emergency or prevent the disclosure of information concerning "security matters."*

The Commerce Department's failure to apply the CoCom controls to South Africa leaves ample room for either South African government consignees, or private end-users to divert equipment to the police or military. The application of the CoCom controls to South Africa would effectively restrict many of the transactions of high-tech equipment cited in this study.

The State Department has refused to make public its administrative guidelines implementing the U.S. embargo against South Africa. The Washington Office on Africa sought release of the guidelines under the Freedom of Information Act but the request was turned down on the grounds that the export guidelines "contain information, the disclosure of which could reasonably be expected to cause damage to the national security of the United States."[32]

The use of a set of secret guidelines rather than the CoCom list, allows licensing officials to exercise what three U.S. legal experts call "broad and unreviewable discretion" over exports to South Africa, which seriously weakens the stated purpose of the embargo.[33]

Once U.S. equipment reaches South Africa, the United States has little control over its destination or how it is used. At least three pieces of legislation — the

South African National Supplies Procurement Act, the Defence Act and the South African Official Secrets Act – permit Pretoria to seize equipment it needs in an emergency, or prevent the disclosure of information concerning "security matters."[34] A similar piece of legislation announced in 1979 laid the groundwork for a government takeover of virtually any computer in South Africa, providing for a mandatory countrywide inventory of all computer installations, both privately and publicly held. Under threat of prosecution, every owner or lessee of computer hardware in the country was required to submit detailed information, including the make and model of the system, its capacity, application, speed and peripheral equipment.[35]

These South African laws make it difficult to determine exactly how U.S. equipment in South Africa is being used. The case of a Philadelphia-owned company helps illustrate this problem. According to a cable from the State Department, released under the Freedom of Information Act, CGS Thermodynamics (Pty.), Ltd., a Johannesburg subsidiary of CGS Scientific Corporation, was implicated in an illegal multimillion dollar scheme to supply electronic equipment to a military or police agency in South Africa. The scheme apparently involved the transshipment of equipment from West Germany. An informant who was interviewed by the U.S. government.in connection with the case stated, "initially that the subject equipment was to be used in the establishment of a semiconductor facility within South Africa." The Commerce Department, said the cable, "has reason to believe that the equipment was diverted to a proscribed destination; however, attempts through a multitude of channels to obtain definitive information and documentation substantiating such a contention have met with largely negative results."[36] Despite the alleged violation, the U.S. government apparently failed to pursue the investigation because of the difficulty in gathering information about the case; no charges have been filed. Since this case arose, CGS has disappeared from the list of U.S. corporations operating in South Africa, published annually by the U.S. consulate in Johannesburg. The company has presumably passed into South African hands, or been withdrawn.

**Clandestine Access:** When the use of third parties and front groups within South Africa, collusion with multinational suppliers, or the manipulation of loopholes in the embargo are not enough to guarantee the supply of needed equipment, the white minority regime has made it clear that it is prepared to engage in clandestine activities to insure its access to crucial foreign technology.

On February 24, 1978 – only eight days after the Commerce Department expanded controls on exports destined for South Africa – a South African negotiator flew to France to try to close an illegal deal for computer parts. The attempt was disclosed by an official at IBM's European headquarters in Orly, who said the South African representative tried to place an order worth "several million dollars" for spare parts. Although IBM's West German subsidiary had previously offered to supply spares to embargoed South African agencies, an official said the company turned down the offer.[37] The same year, a South African electronics journal reported that the regime's police and military were "obtaining supplies from back-door sources overseas . . ."[38]

Information provided by a confidential South African source indicates that the South Africans remove company names and identifying marks from illegally acquired computers to make it more difficult to trace their origins.

# SUMMARY

It is evident that the existing embargo has not prevented strategic technology from reaching South Africa, and, once there, from being put at the disposal of repressive agencies. Pretoria is well-positioned to violate the embargo with impunity: The white regime can acquire U.S. computers, electronics and other equipment under false pretenses and use them as instruments of repression as it sees fit. The South African regime has a range of laws at its disposal to frustrate enforcement of the embargo and it can simply commandeer any equipment it cannot get through other channels.

On the surface, Washington's failure to stop the flow of high-tech equipment to the South African regime indicates a weakness in U.S. *policy*. While this is true, the failure of the ban also stems from something deeper than a set of inadequate regulations. To date, the U.S. government has not exhibited the fundamental *political will* necessary to make the embargo stick. This problem is compounded by the fact that U.S. multinationals are deeply involved with the white power structure, and are committed to helping it adjust to the threat posed by trade sanctions.

Failure is built in to the embargo, as it is presently defined, because it is only a partial ban, covering only a few commodities outright (weapons, for example), and only a very few agencies of the South African government. These structrual flaws, combined with lax enforcement on the part of the U.S. government, virtually guarantee that the embargo will not live up to its purpose. The State Department and the Commerce Department may have issued the regulations establishing the embargo. But in reality, U.S. corporations, and their subsidiaries — worldwide and in South Africa — are setting the actual operating parameters of the embargo. The corporations have accomplished this, among other methods, by making plans to switch to non-U.S. supply stocks and pledging to help Pretoria overcome any potential shortages of strategic goods by deceptive means — both as revealed in State Department documents released for this study.

### Recommendations

Given the weaknesses of the present embargo and the regime's ability to circumvent it, the only way to deny Pretoria access to strategic technology is for

*"Illegal" squatters' camp at Cross Roads. United Nations/P. Magubane*

U.S. companies to disengage from South Africa and for the U.S. government to place a total ban on the sale of U.S. strategic and dual-use equipment there. Possible interim steps toward this more comprehensive embargo include:

1) An immediate ban on the sale and lease of all equipment to the South African government, including all agencies and semi-government bodies.

2) A requirement that prohibits any exports to South Africa, unless the U.S. exporter can demonstrate that the commodity under question has no potential military or repressive applications, and unless the South African consignee will allow U.S. government representatives to monitor the use of the commodity.

3) An extension of the embargo to cover all services and products sold to South Africa from U.S. subsidiaries in third countries.

4) An extension of the embargo to cover sales of equipment to foreign-owned manufacturers who re-sell to South Africa with provisions for inspections.

5) An immediate ban on the sale to South Africa of any commodity on the CoCom list, or any commodity that carries a "QPL", "mil-spec" or related designation.

6) An extension of the embargo to cover strategically important technical information, know-how, training and similar transactions.

7) Rigorous enforcement, including the creation of an infrastructure to monitor compliance which involves licensing officials, U.S. Customs officers, U.S. diplomatic personnel; also including provisions for regular reports to Congress and the United Nations on the status of U.S. observance of the embargo.

## Insuring Compliance With the Embargo

Multilateral action is necessary to insure that the embargo is consistently interpreted, applied and observed around the world. The U.S. government has secured consensus from most of its allies on restricting high-tech sales to the Soviet Union and Eastern Europe. This precedent could easily be applied to South Africa. International cooperation is imperative if a real embargo is to be effective. The United Nations could play a leading role by setting specific, internationally recognized guidelines for the embargo; by outlining specific steps for implementing the embargo; and by monitoring member nations' compliance on an ongoing basis.[39]

*... public scrutiny and involvement are critical to the success of the embargo.*

However important rigorous enforcement of the embargo by governments and international bodies may be, public scrutiny and involvement are critical to the success of the embargo. The corporations are sensitive to public opinion. As more details about their business with the Pretoria regime come to light, the multinationals will face rising opposition from people in this country who take offense at their tacit alliance with white supremacy in South Africa. Increasing numbers of colleges, churches and religious groups, state legislatures, municipal councils and trade unions are pressing the multinationals to release information about their business with the South African government, and demanding that they withdraw.

The labor movement also has an important role to play in expanding and enforcing the embargo. British unionists performed an invaluable service by revealing the planned sale of ICL computers to the South African police and trying to stop it. Dutch electronics workers at Philips facilities in Holland are

*Primary school children at Cross Roads. United Nations/P. Magubane*

beginning to question their company's sales to the apartheid government. Early in February 1982, the Dutch trade federation issued a public call to the Dutch government, urging that all sales to Pretoria's security forces be halted.[40] Both white- and blue-collar electronics workers in the United States (and those at U.S.-owned subsidiaries in third countries that supply South Africa) are in a unique position to expose and challenge the role of U.S. multinationals in automating apartheid. Far too little information is available about computer and electronics sales to Pretoria. The disclosure of planned sales and shipments of U.S. high-tech equipment to South Africa by concerned workers would help widen the debate and act as a catalyst by opening U.S. corporate dealings with Pretoria up to public scrutiny.

U.S. computer and electronics multinationals that trade with South Africa have yet to feel the full weight of public opinion. In the spring of 1980, Hewlett-Packard Chair, David Packard, presided over a groundbreaking ceremony for the new Hewlett-Packard headquarters in Johannesburg and used the occasion to criticize groups in the United States calling for divestment. The Nebraska legislature had recently decided to dispose of its holdings in U.S. companies operating in South Africa. " . . . Some states back home say they intend to boycott U.S. companies which trade with South Africa. Well, that doesn't worry us at all . . . I'd much rather lose business with Nebraska than with South Africa," he said.[41] Packard's flash of candor and arrogance was unusual. Corporate chiefs are generally more circumspect in public, even when answering criticism about collaboration with South Africa. Unfortunately, the commitment to Pretoria reflected in Packard's remark is shared by the industry at large and it is likely to flourish under the Reagan Administration's relaxed embargo. The flow of advanced technology from the United States to Pretoria is a shameful manifestation of complicity with white minority rule. It bolsters apartheid and it stands as a challenge to all who want democracy and peace for South Africa.

*After majority rule comes to South Africa, we might see a museum depicting what life under apartheid was like – much like the memorials at concentration camps and similar museums one sees today in West and East Germany and elsewhere. These places display the Nazi ledgers bearing the names of the persecuted. They show maps of the ghettoes, photos of terrified victims, instruments of torture, and they list the names of scientists and companies who lent their services to the Nazi government.*

*A museum of this kind in a free South Africa will be similar in some respects, different in others. Its walls will bear charts explaining how the minority government used to control blacks, Indians and Asians by means of racial zoning and a system of "homelands."*

*Banned books will be on display, along with pictures of people who were* banned, driven into exile or prison, and killed. *The artifacts of repression and state terror will be on exhibit, and the museum will show how foreign companies supported apartheid. Next to a "sjambok" police whip used against demonstrators will be a "hippo" riot vehicle and cannisters of tear gas. Another exhibit will show how private police, who went through a training program developed in the United States, were used to put down strikes.*

*Visiting school children will be able to view the technology that so fascinated the former white-controlled government. Those who have never seen a "passbook" or "Book of Life" will file past a display with the IBM 370 and ICL computers that Pretoria used for its automated population register. An exhibit about the "Bantu Administration Boards" – long since abolished – will show how computers from NCR, Mohawk and Burroughs streamlined the agencies' work.*

*The shell of a deadly missile cut away to show its electronic innards will reveal U.S. components – perhaps from TRW, Westinghouse, RCA, Motorola or any of dozens of other companies. A guide will tell visitors how local institutes and companies that developed weapons for Pretoria's arsenal got access to hardware from Control Data, Burroughs, IBM and Hewlett-Packard.*

*The museum will be a memorial to all those who resisted and suffered under white rule, and an indictment of all who collaborated with it.*

# NOTES AND DOCUMENTATION

## CHAPTER ONE

1. *The Boston Globe*, February 28, 1982.
2. Seidman, Ann and Neva, *South Africa and U.S. Multinational Corporations*, Westport, CT: Lawrence Hill and Co., 1978, p. 26.
3. *Johannesburg Star*, September 24, 1980.
4. Friedman, Julian, R. *Basic Facts On the Republic of South Africa and the Policy of Apartheid*, United Nations: U.N. Centre Against Apartheid, March, 1977, p. 46.
5. *Survey of Race Relations in South Africa 1979*, Johannesburg: South African Institute of Race Relations, p. 197.
6. See for example, *Christian Science Monitor*, April 14, 1981.
7. Background briefing paper released by Transafrica, Washington, D.C.
8. CBS News, March 3, 1981.
9. *Wall Street Journal*, April 15, 1981.
10. Seidman, p. 80.
11. *Current Business*, August, 1980, p. 27.
12. "Imports of Minerals from South Africa by the United States and by OECD Countries." Congressional Research Service, Library of Congress, Report prepared for the Subcommittee on African Affairs of the Committee on Foreign Relations, U.S. Senate, September, 1980.

## CHAPTER TWO

1. *Sunday Times,* Business Times, March 26, 1978.
2. *South African Computer Users Handbook*, Johannesburg: Systems Publishers, 1980, p. A30 (Cited hereafter as *CUH*).
3. Ibid, A30.
4. Cockbain, T.G.E., "Radar development in South Africa with special reference to air defence," *The Transactions of the S.A. Institute of Electrical Engineers*, April 1979, p. 88.
5. *CUH*, 1980, p. A33.
6. Mackenzie, Peter, "Computers – the extra hands of the eighties," *Management*, December 1980, p. 48.
7. Orphen, Stephen, "The chip revolution," *Management*, December 1979, pp. 49-50.
8. Ibid.
9. Ibid.
10. Ibid., p. 49.
11. "South Africa Review Service – International Business Machines Corporation," Investor Responsibility Research Center (Hereafter IRRC), Washington, D.C., June 1981, p. 3.
12. IRRC, p. 1.
13. Purvis, Gail, "South Africa on upswing despite embargoes," *Datamation*, June 1979, p. 194X.

14. Koenderman, Tony, "Computers take a byte," *Management,* December 1978, p. 56.
15. Orphen, pp. 49-50.
16. Koenderman, p. 59.
17. Firms are from *CUH,* 1980 and *CUH,* 1981.
18. Koenderman, p. 45.
19. Ibid.
20. Purvis, p. 194T.
21. Mehlman, J. Maxwell, Milch, Thomas H. and Toumanoff, Michael V., "United States restrictions on exports to South Africa," *The American Journal of International Law,* October 1979, p. 591.
22. *Export Administration Regulations,* (Cited hereafter as *EAR*), U.S. Department of Commerce, October 1980. The most relevant parts are: 373.1; 379.4; 385.4; Supplement 2 to 285, and Supplement 2 to 379. Munitions control regulations, which cover the export of weapons, are under the cognizance of the State Department.
23. *EAR,* Supplement 2 to Part 385.
24. Myers, Desaix, III, *U.S. Business in South Africa,* Bloomington: Investor Responsibility Research Center, 1980, p. 205.
25. U.S. Embassy, Pretoria, Cable to Secretary of State, October 13, 1978.
26. U.S. Consulate, Johannesburg, Cable to Secretary of State, June 9, 1978.
27. Ibid.
28. American Chamber of Commerce in South Africa, Correspondence to Office of Export Administration, U.S. Department of Commerce, February 5, 1981.
29. Secretary of State, Cable to U.S. Embassy, Johannesburg, September 21, 1978.
30. Control Data Corporation, Correspondence to Office of Export Administration, U.S. Department of Commerce, March 9, 1981.
31. *Federal Register,* June 30, 1981, p. 33509. The change also permitted the sale of medical supplies to the military and police.
32. *Africa News,* December 7, 1981.
33. "Export Controls for Foreign Policy Purposes Extended for the Period March 1, 1982, through January 29, 1983." Draft copy of regulations obtained from Congressional source.
34. U.S. Department of Commerce, Interview with AFSC, March 5, 1982.

## CHAPTER THREE

1. *The Apartheid War Machine,* International Defence and Aid Fund, London 1980, p. 5.
2. Department of Defence, *White Paper on Defence* (Hereafter, *White Paper*), Pretoria, March 29, 1977.
3. See Mehlman, et al, p. 589.
4. Department of Plural Relations, *Annual Report,* Pretoria, 1977.
5. Office of the Scientific Adviser to the Prime Minister, *National Register of Service-Rendering Information Centres and of Data Banks,* Pretoria, July 1979, pp. 4-5.
6. Ibid.
7. South African Bureau of National and International Communication, *Official Yearbook of the Republic of South Africa,* (Cited hereafter as *Yearbook*), Pretoria, 1979, p. 286.
8. Atonement Friars, Notes from meeting with IBM representatives, April 10, 1975.
9. *New York Times,* January 15, 1981.
10. "IBM Operations in South Africa," Paper from IBM, March, 1979.
11. Department of the Interior and Immigration, *Annual Report,* Pretoria, 1978, p. 7.
12. *Yearbook,* p. 162.
13. Department of Bantu Administration and Development, annual report, 1975/76.

# 80

14. Department of Plural Affairs and Development, annual report, 1977/78, p. 29.
15. Ibid.
16. *Financial Mail,* March 24, 1978.
17. Ibid.
18. *Data World*, Auerbach Publishers (U.S.), undated.
19. *Yearbook*, p. 229.
20. *Municipal Administration and Engineering,* December, 1979, p. 14.
21. Information regarding computer installations is taken from the "S.A. Computer Users Guide," a survey of computers, published annually in *Management* in November or December. Issues used in this study are from 1977 through 1980; they will be cited hereafter as *Management*. Other sources used are *CUH*, 1980 and *CUH*, 1981.
22. *CUH*, 1980.
23. *Survey of Race Relations in South Africa 1979*, Johannesburg: South African Institute of Race Relations, p. 420.
24. *CUH*, 1980.
25. *Survey of Race Relations in South Africa*, p. 420.
26. *CUH*, 1981.
27. *Survey of Race Relations in South Africa*, p. 389.
28. *Johannesburg Star,* November 10, 1980.
29. "South Africa Review Service – Control Data Corporation," IRRC, Washington, D.C., February 1981, p. 16.
30. *CUH*, 1980; *CUH*, 1981; *Management*, 1977-1980.
31. The State Tender Board is a statutory body under the Department of Finance which handles procurement for several agencies. For more information, see *Yearbook, 1979,* p. 156, and issues of the *State Tender Bulletin.*
32. The examples of transactions were taken from several issues of the *State Tender Bulletin*, from September 1980 through March 1981.
33. *Survey of Race Relations in South Africa*, op cit, p. 450. Since this incident, the council has agreed to consider requests for use of the hall on a permit basis only, according to the Race Relations Survey.
34. *Municipal Administration and Engineering,* April 1980.
35. *CUH*, 1980.
36. "SAMRAS S.A. Municipal Receipting and Accounting System," NCR-South Africa, undated.
37. Claassen, P.E. Dr., "Computers in local government," *Municipal Administration and Engineering*, June 1980, p. 7.
38. *Paratus,* South African Defence Force, Pretoria, October 1979.
39. Cassidy, Gerry (Control Data Pty. Ltd.), "Computer-aided designing," *Public Works/ Openbare Werke*, February 1980, pp. 35-37.
40. Conrad, Thomas (NARMIC/American Friends Service Committee) "Automating Apartheid: U.S. Electronics and Computer Support for South Africa's Apartheid Government," Paper presented at the International Seminar on the Implementation and Reinforcement of the Arms Embargo Against South Africa, London, April 1-3 1981, p. 13.
41. *Public Works/Openbare Werke,* February 1980, p. 36.
42. Mare, Gerry, *African Population Relocation in South Africa,* Johannesburg: S.A. Institute of Race Relations, p. 28. "Hippos" are riot-control vehicles; the sneeze machine is an anti-riot device that spews out repellant gas.
43. See, e.g. Maré, op cit. p. 35.
44. *CUH*, 1980.

**CHAPTER FOUR**
1. Figures are from *The Military Balance*, London: The International Institute for Strategic Studies, 1980-1981, p. 54. For additional background, see also *The Apartheid War Machine*, op cit and Frankel, Philip H., "South Africa - The politics of police control," *Comparative Politics*, New York: The City University of New York, July 1980.
2. Stockwell, John, *In Search of Enemies – A CIA Story*, as quoted in *U.S. Military Involvement in Southern Africa*, "Covert Operations in Central and Southern Africa," by James Dingeman, Boston: South End Press, 1978, p. 90. BOSS, The Bureau of State Security, was the predecessor of the National Intelligence Service.
3. RSO, Pretoria, Memorandum to Chief SY/FO, September 14, 1971.
4. *SARP Magazine for the South African Police*, January 1976, p. 14.
5. Klare, Michael T. and Arnson, Cynthia, *Supplying Repression, U.S. Support for Authoritarian Regimes Abroad*, Washington, D.C.: Institute for Policy Studies, 1981, p. 33.
6. *New York Times*, November 6, 1976.
7. *The Police Chief*, "Directory of IACP Members," October 1979; *Africa News*, January 18, 1982.
8. *Sunday Express*, January 13, 1980.
9. *Management*, December 1978.
10. *Computing* (UK), August 17, 1978.
11. *Datalink* (UK), April 9, 1978.
12. Unless otherwise noted, all information regarding the ICL/Control Data deal is from *St. Louis Post Dispatch*, March 10, 1979.
13. Department of State, Cable to U.S. Embassy, London, May 18, 1979.
14. U.S. Commerce Department, Interview with AFSC, September 9, 1981; information about the penalty against ICL is from a Commerce Department press release, March 3, 1982 and from background materials provided by the Department.
15. *Data World*, op cit.
16. *ICL, Ltd. Annual Report and Accounts*, 1980, p. 6.
17. *St. Louis Post Dispatch*, March 10, 1979.
18. *Servamus*, South African Police, April 1980, p. 17.
19. Ibid.
20. "United Electronics launches new two-way system," *Electronics and Instrumentation* (Hereafter cited as *E&I*), April 1979, p. 65.
21. *Rand Daily Mail*, May 4, 1979.
22. Anderson, Jack, "Embargo on South Africa called farce," *The Washington Post*, May 30, 1981, p. E51.
23. RCA, Correspondence to AFSC, March 20, 1981.
24. RCA, Interview with AFSC, December 24, 1980.
25. RCA, Correspondence to AFSC, March 20, 1981.
26. See Mehlman, et al, pp. 593 and 596.
27. RCA, Correspondence to AFSC, June 15, 1981.
28. IBM outlines its policy in a company paper, "IBM Operations in South Africa," op cit.
29. *CUH*, 1980.
30. IBM, Correspondence to AFSC, March 11, 1981.

31. Conrad, "Automating Apartheid," p. 15.
32. Anderson, op cit.
33. IBM, Correspondence to AFSC, May 11, 1981.
34. IBM, Interview with AFSC, June 19, 1981.
35. *CUH*, 1980.
36. IBM, Interview with AFSC, June 19, 1981.
37. "All Things Considered," National Public Radio, June 20, 1981.
38. Conradie, W.A.C. Commandant, and Peters, A. Commandant, "Total security," *Armed Forces*, June 1981.
39. "The Security Association of South Africa," Descriptive Memo, undated.
40. "The treasurehouse of Africa," *Security and Protection of SA*, February 1978.
41. "American Firms, Subsidiaries and Affiliates - South Africa," American Consulate General, Johannesburg, September 1980.
42. Mine Safety's sales to Iran and Colombia taken from Klare and Arnson, pp. 144 and 146.
43. *Security and Protection of SA*, March/April 1978, p. 8.
44. *Security and Protection of SA*, February 1978.
45. *E&I*, November 1978.
46. TCI's sales to the Pentagon are listed in *Contract Quarterly*, Greenwich, CT: Defense Marketing Service. July-September 1979, p. 560 and April-June 1980, p. 494.
47. *Municipal Administration and Engineering*, September 1978, p. 18.
48. *Municipal Administration and Engineering*, July 1978, p. 79.
49. *Security and Protection of SA*, May/June 1978.
50. An early look at passive infrared applications during Vietnam came in *Air Force Magazine* (US), July 1968, p. 34.
51. *E&I*, op cit, February 1979, p. 80. During the Vietnam War, a major share of Barnes' business was with the Pentagon and large military contractors. According to the Defense Marketing Service ("Market Intelligence Report - Aerospace Companies," September 1970), equipment from the company was used in a range of ground-based and ground-to-air weapons systems. Barnes also worked on *Project Shed Light*, an Air Force night detection system.
52. Barnes Engineering, Interview with AFSC, September 29, 1981.
53. *Financial Mail*, July 11, 1980, p. 132.
54. *Security and Protection of SA*, February 1978 and October 1980, p. 32.
55. *Security and Protection of SA*, February 1978.
56. *Security and Protection of SA*, May/June 1978.
57. *Security and Protection of SA*, January/February 1978.
58. *The Police Chief*, October 1979, p. 251.
59. *Security and Protection of SA*, January/February 1978.
60. *Security and Protection of SA*, October 1980.
61. See "Export Controls for Foreign Policy Purposes Extended for the Period March 1, 1982 through January 20, 1983," op cit.
62. IACP, Interview with AFSC, March 3, 1982 and published materials provided by the IACP.
63. "CASS Crime Analysis System Support," Product information sheet published by the IACP, undated; also "CASS: New Weapon in War on Crime," Report prepared by Prince William Police Department, Manassas, Virginia, undated.
64. IACP, Interview with AFSC, March 3, 1982.
65. Laucher, John W., "Small Computers and Criminal Justice," Paper prepared for Criminal Justice Information and Statistics Systems International Search Symposium, 1979. Quote is from an abstract provided by the National Criminal Justice Reference

Service, Rockville MD, March 17, 1982.
66. *Proceedings, Carnahan Conference on Crime Countermeasures*, Lexington: University of Kentucky, May 16-18, 1979; also "Jams - Jail Accounting Microcomputer System Demonstration of a New Technology," Sacramento, CA: Search Group Inc., 1978. Both as abstracted by the National Criminal Justice Reference Service, ibid.

## CHAPTER FIVE

1. Information about weapons developments is from *South African Digest*, May 9, 1980, p. 1.
2. *The Washington Post*, July 7, 1981.
3. *The Apartheid War Machine*, p. 10.
4. *New York Times*, August 13, 1981.
5. *The Apartheid War Machine*, p. 9.
6. *The Military Balance*, op cit. 1980-1981, p. 54. These figures do not include the ranks of the police establishment.
7. For additional information about South Africa's military, see *The Apartheid War Machine*, especially chapters 3, 4, 5 and 8.
8. Gervassi, Sean, "South Africa's War in Namibia," unpublished manuscript, undated, p. 39.
9. Jacobs, K.E. "DISA: 'Blommetjie' met 'n ystervuis!" *Paratus*, January 1976, p. 26.
10. *Management*, December 1973.
11. *Management*, December 1974.
12. All information about DISA is from Jacobs, pp. 26-28.
13. Unless otherwise noted, all information about Project Konvoor is from "Die Weermag Bespaar Miljoene — Met Projek Konvoor," *Paratus*, August 1977.
14. Information about computer use by the Northern Logistics Command and quote are from "Stille Werkers Agter de Skerms," *Paratus*, May 1978, Supplement V.
15. *Paratus*, op cit, August 1977 and Purvis, June 1979, p. 194CC.
16. IBM, Correspondence to AFSC, February 13, 1981.
17. "Some technical uses of computers," *E&I*, August 1978, pp. 7-9.
18. *Paratus*, May 1978.
19. *E&I*, August 1978, pp. 7-9.
20. Lord Carrington, Correspondence to Abdul Minty, September 3, 1979; see also *Daily Telegraph* (UK) August 3, 1979 and *The Guardian* (UK) September 5, 1979.
21. Digital Equipment International Ltd., Correspondence to Irish Anti-Apartheid Movement, September 4, 1979.
22. Secretary of State, Cable to U.S. Embassy, London, August 3, 1979.
23. Abdul Minty, Cable to Secretary of State, May 5, 1981.
24. *Computing* (UK), August 31, 1978.
25. *CUH*, 1981.
26. IBM, Correspondence to AFSC, February 13, 1981.
27. Information about the satellite-based system in this section, unless otherwise noted, is taken from Braham, Harold S. Dr. (General Electric Company, USA) "Satellite communication to mobiles," *E&I*, April 1979, pp. 49-50; p. 52.
28. Information about GE's tests of the application of this system for crime control is from *Proceedings, 1977 Carnahan Conference on Crime Countermeasures*, Lexington: University of Kentucky, April 6-8, 1977.
29. Information about the agreement with NASA for the satellite stations and the military tracking station is from *South Africa: Time Running Out, The Report of the Study Commission on U.S. Policy Toward Southern Africa*, Berkeley: Foreign Policy Study Foundation, Inc., 1981, p. 347.

30. NASA, Interview with AFSC, March 13, 1981.
31. Information about Silvermine is from *The Apartheid War Machine*, p. 32 and *The Wall Street Journal*, July 31, 1975, p. 26.
32. List of manufacturers indicated in Advokaat documents, undated memorandum, Washington Office on Africa.
33. *The Wall Street Journal*, July 31, 1975, p. 26.
34. Ibid.
35. Ibid and *The Apartheid War Machine*, p. 33.
36. Vayrynen, Raimo, "The role of transnational corporations in the military sector of South Africa," *Journal of Southern Africa Affairs*, Brunswick, OH: Southern Africa Research Association, April 1980, p. 222.
37. *White Paper*, 1979, p. 23.
38. *Salvo*, as quoted in *The Apartheid War Machine*, p. 16.
39. *Financial Mail*, May 25, 1979, p. 683.
40. *White Paper*, p. 23.
41. *Yearbook*, 1978, p. 708.
42. *Financial Mail*, May 25, 1979, p. 683.
43. *White Paper*, 1979, pp. 24-25.
44. *Financial Mail*, May 25, 1979, p. 683.
45. Beaumont, Tony, "Local manufacture necessary for strategic reasons – a review," *E&I*, January 1979, p. 24.
46. *CUH*, 1974.
47. Ibid.
48. "Computers: where, what and when," *Management*, November 1974.
49. *EAR*, Supplement 2 to Part 385, October 1, 1980.
50. *Sunday Times*, Business Times, March 26, 1978.
51. *The Apartheid War Machine*, p. 16.
52. *Africa News*, op cit, December 7, 1981; *Boston Globe*, February 28, 1982.
53. *Yearbook*, p. 708.
54. *Council for Scientific and Industrial Research* (Hereafter CSIR), *1979 Annual Report*, Pretoria, April 1, 1980. See pp. 3-29.
55. Stack, Louise and Morton, Don, *Torment to Triumph in Southern Africa*, New York, NY: Friendship Press, 1976, p. 42.
56. *The Apartheid War Machine*, p. 15.
57. Milton, D.N.A., "Application of digital signal processing to military systems," *The Transactions of the S.A. Institute of Electrical Engineers*, op cit, May 1980, p. 128.
58. *Servamus*, March 1981.
59. All information about the activities of CSIR subsidiaries outlined in this paper, unless otherwise noted, are from the 1978, 1979 and 1980 annual reports of the respective institute or lab.
60. CSIR, *Centre for Computing Services Annual Report*, 1978/79, Pretoria, September 1979, p. 11.
61. *The Apartheid War Machine*, p. 15.
62. See for example Rubin, O.H. "Design of feedback control systems," *The Transactions of the S.A. Institute of Electrical Engineers*, July 1977, p. 148; also Milton, D.N.A. op cit, p. 128; and Engelbrecht, J.F., "Application of surface acoustic wave devices," *The Transactions of the S.A. Institute of Electrical Engineers*, November, 1980, pp. 320-330.
63. *Paratus*, October 1981, p. 98.
64. *White Paper*, 1979, pp. 24-25.
65. *Debates*, April 17, 1978, quoted from *The Apartheid War Machine*, p. 15.
66. IBM, Correspondence to AFSC, February 13, 1981.

67. "Export Controls for Foreign Policy Purposes Extended for the Period March 1, 1982, through January 20, 1983," op cit.
68. *CUII*, 1980; *CUH*, 1981; Vayrynen, p. 215.
69. *CUH*, 1980; *CUH*, 1981.
70. *CUH*, 1981; *Reply*, p. 30; *Paratus*, August 1977.
71. Vayrynen, p. 217.
72. *CUH*, 1981.
73. *CUH*, 1981; *National Register*, p. 126 and p. 131; *Paratus*, June 1981, p. 51 and May 1981, p. 20.
74. "Ons soldate kyk vyand vreesloos in die oe," *Paratus*, September 1979, p. 25; *Servamus*, July 1980; *CUH*, 1981.
75. Albrecht, Ulrich, "A Definition of Arms and Related Material," Paper presented at the International Seminar on the Implementation and Reinforcement of the Arms Embargo Against South Africa, London, April 1-3, 1981, pp. 5 and 9-10.
76. *E&I*, October 1978, p. 72.
77. NARMIC, "The Defense Department's Top 100," September 1981.
78. *E&I*, December 1978.
79. *E&I*, May 1979.
80. *Armed Forces*, October 1977, p. 25.
81. *The Transactions of the S.A. Institute of Electrical Engineers*, Johannesburg: February 1981, p. 44; see also Kistler *General Catalog* K2.004 (undated) and Technical Data Sheet Quartz High Pressure Transducer Type 6213 (undated) from Kistler.
82. Unless otherwise stated, information in this section about Philips and its U.S. subsidiaries is from "The Philips Connection - Military Electronics for South Africa," Netherlands Anti-Apartheid Movement, October 1980.
83. *E&I*, June 1979.
84. *Sunday Times* (UK), July 24, 1977.
85. Beaumont, p. 25.
86. *Sunday Times* (UK), July 24, 1977.
87. NARMIC, "The Defense Department's Top 100."
88. "Contracting DMS Intelligence," Defense Marketing Service, April 1, 1981, p. 2.
89. *Contract Quarterly*, Greenwich, CT: Defense Marketing Service, July-September 1980, p. 330.
90. "Contracting DMS Intelligence," February 13, 1981, p. 9.
91. "Contracting DMS Intelligence," January 15, 1981, p. 10.
92. *Contract Quarterly*, July-September 1980, p. 330.
93. "Contracting DMS Intelligence," April 17, 1981, p. 10.
94. Beaumont, Tony, "Altech, six months after . . . " *E&I*, April 1978, p. 7.
95. *E&I*, April 1979, p. 3.
96. *Financial Times*, Tuesday, September 16, 1980.
97. Beaumont, *E&I*, April 1978, p. 7.
98. *Financial Times* (UK), November 28, 1980; Beaumont, Tony, "Arms embargo influence for '78," *E&I*, December 1978, p. 31.
99. Beaumont, Tony, *E&I*, April 1978, p. 7.

## CHAPTER SIX

1. *Federal Register*, January 8, 1980, announcement from the Department of Commerce.
2. Beaumont, Tony, *E&I*, December 1978, p. 29.
3. *Sunday Times*, April 22, 1979.
4. Purvis, Gail, *Datamation*, June 1979, p. 194X.
5. *CUH*, 1981, p. A1.

6. Office of the Scientific Adviser to the Prime Minister, *National Register of Service-Rendering Information Centres and of Data Banks*, op cit.
7. Ibid.
8. *Sunday Times*, Business Times, March 26, 1978.
9. *Electronic News Financial Factbook*, New York: 1979.
10. *CUH*, 1980.
11. Nadel, Laurie and Wiener, Hesh, "Would you sell a computer to Hitler?" *Computer Decisions*, January 1977, p. 23.
12. Orphen, Stephen, *Management*, December 1979, p. 50.
13. "Perseus forge Itel link," *E&I*, February 1979, p. 21; National Semiconductor, Interview with AFSC, March 1981; Itel, Interview with AFSC, March 1981.
14. Orphen, Stephen, *Management*, December 1979, p. 50.
15. U.S. Embassy, Pretoria, Cable to Secretary of State, October 13, 1978.
16. IBM, Correspondence to AFSC, February 13, 1981.
17. American Embassy, Pretoria, Cable to Secretary of State, August 1, 1979.
18. Mehlman, Milch and Toumanoff, p. 593.
19. IBM, Correspondence to AFSC, February 13, 1981.
20. Information about the NPRL's activities is from CSIR, *Annual Report July 1979-June 1980*, (National Physical Research Laboratory) op cit.
21. *CUH*, 1980, p. B10.
22. For a look at Plato's use by the U.S. Air Force, see Control Data's advertisement in *Air Force Magazine*, November, 1981, p. 97; Plato's use in police training is outlined in "Plato Teaches Cops," in the *Illinois Police Officer*, Spring 1979, pp. 103-117.
23. *Paratus*, May 1981, p. 67.
24. Ibid.
25. *Servamus*, July 1980.
26. "Philips 50 Years in South Africa - Serving Industry," as quoted in "The Philips Connection - Military Electronics for South Africa," op cit, p. 11.
27. Purvis, Gail, "South Africa on upswing despite embargoes," *Datamation*, op cit, p. 194CC.
28. Ibid.
29. Examples of software programs available in South Africa from Control Data are from: Cassidy, Gerry (Control Data Pty. Ltd.), *Public Works/Openbare Werke*, op cit, and the following product literature received from Control Data: "Control Data Cybernet Services: AnSys - Engineering Analysis System," undated; "SimSci Process Simulation Program," undated; "Control Data Corporation Cybernet Shipping Services" undated; "The British Ship Research Association," undated.
30. *The Philadelphia Bulletin*, August 20, 1981.
31. *EAR*, Commodity Control List and Part 399.
32. Undated draft of press release, Washington Office on Africa p. 1.
33. Mehlman, Milch and Toumanoff, p. 592.
34. Mehlman, Milch and Toumanoff, pp. 593 and 596.
35. Department of Statistics, "Regulation No. 1166," published in *Government Gazette*, Pretoria, June 8, 1979.
36. Department of State, Cable to American Consulate, Frankfurt, July 18, 1978.
37. *Electronic News* (US), March 6, 1978.
38. Beaumont, Tony, "Arms embargo influence for '78," *E&I*, December 1978, p. 29.
39. The International Seminar on the Implementation and Reinforcement of the Arms Embargo Against South Africa held in London early in April 1981 was one effort to build support within the United Nations for expanding the embargo. This gathering was convened by the United Nations Special Committee Against Apartheid and the

World Campaign Against Military and Nuclear Collaboration With South Africa.
40. "Verklaring Over Nederlandse Naleving Van Het Verplichte Wapenembargo Tegen Zuid-Afrika" (Declaration Concerning the Netherlands' Compliance With the Mandatory Arms Embargo Against South Africa), Federation of Dutch Trade Unions (FNV) and the Dutch Anti-Apartheid Movement, February 8, 1982.
41. Packard is quoted from U.S. Consulate, Johannesburg, Cable to Secretary of State, April 17, 1980. His remarks were also covered in the U.S. trade press.

## VI. NOTES FOR APPENDIX SIX

1. *The Apartheid War Machine*, p. 15.
2. Rubin, O.H., "Design of feedback control systems," *The Transactions of the S.A. Institute of Electrical Engineers*, July 1977, p. 148.
3. Milton, D.N.A., p. 128.
4. Engelbrecht, J.F., "Application of surface acoustic wave devices," *The Transactions of the S.A. Institute of Electrical Engineers*, November 1980, pp. 320-330.
5. Malherbe, J.A.G., "Miniature wideband filters for hybrid system applications," *The Transactions of the S.A. Institute of Electrical Engineers*, February 1980, p. 38.
6. *Management*, November 1974.
7. *EAR*, Supplement 2 to Part 384.
8. *Yearbook*, p. 514.
9. CSIR, *1979 Annual Report*, p. 49.
10. *Paratus*, October 1981, p. 98.
11. Information about the NIAST's access to Control Data and Perkin-Elmer hardware is from CSIR, *Centre for Computing Services Annual Report 1979/1980*, Pretoria, September 1980.
12. CSIR, *National Research Institute for Mathematical Sciences Annual Report 1979/1980*, Pretoria, September 1980.
13. CSIR, *NMERI Annual Report 1980*, Pretoria, October 1980; CSIR, *Annual Report 1980* (National Chemical Research Laboratory), 1980.
14. CSIR, *1979 Annual Report*, p. 11.
15. CSIR, *Annual Report June 1980* (National Accelerator Centre); for further discussion and background on South Africa's nuclear capability, see: Walters, Ronald W., "U.S. Policy and Nuclear Proliferation: South Africa," in *U.S. Military Involvement in Southern Africa*, op cit; also: Lamperti, John, "Nuclear South Africa: Background and Prospects," NARMIC, 1979; Clark, Dan, "Military and Nuclear Collaboration with South Africa," World Campaign Against Military and Nuclear Collaboration With South Africa, 1980.
16. "Monitor," Third Channel, broadcast November 20, 1979, transcript reprinted in *Reply – Answer to a Denial of the Government of the Federal Republic of Germany Concerning the Military-Nuclear Collaboration Between the Federal Republic of Germany and South Africa*, Bonn: Anti-Apartheid-Bewegung, December 1979, pp. 128-130.
17. See ibid for additional background.
18. CSIR, *Annual Report 1979/80* (National Electrical Engineering Research Institute), Pretoria, 1980. NEERI also uses software programs from the United States such as SPICE 2 from the University of California at Berkeley; others include SYSCAP II, SIMPIL, MOTIS, GAELIC and TEGAS, according to the Institute's 1979/80 annual report.
19. CSIR, *NITR Annual Report 1978/1979*, (National Institute for Telecommunications Research), Pretoria, 1979.
20. *Management*, December 1978 and December 1979.

21. Cockbain, p. 93.
22. CSIR, *Annual Report July 1979 - June 1980*, (National Physical Research Laboratory), Pretoria, 1980.
23. Olsen, G.H., Nuese, C.J. and Smith, R.T., "The effect of elastic strain on energy band gap and lattice parameter in III-V compounds," *Journal of Applied Physics*, American Institutes of Physics, 1978, p. 5523.
24. See for instance, *IEEE Journal of Quantum Electronics*, August 1979 and *Applied Physics Letters*, February 15, 1979, for examples of work Olsen has done under contract to the U.S. Department of Defense.
25. See for example, *DMS Contract Quarterly*, Greenwich, CT: Defense Marketing Service, July/August/September 1978, p. 668.

# MAJOR U.S. COMPUTER COMPANIES IN SOUTH AFRICA

**CONTROL DATA CORPORATION**
8100 34th Avenue
South Minneapolis, MN 10017
**LOCAL SUBSIDIARY**
Control Data (Pty.) Ltd.
P.O. Box 78105
Sandton 2146
**Number of employes in South Africa:** 250
**Products and services available in South Africa:** a full range of computers in the mainframe and mini series; peripheral equipment; disk storage; computer security equipment; process control devices; encoders; a wide range of electronic components; software; training; consultant services; computer-aided design systems; computer bureau services.

**BURROUGHS CORPORATION**
P.O. Box 418
Detroit, MI 48232
**LOCAL SUBSIDIARY**
Burroughs Machines Ltd.
P.O. Box 3996
Johannesburg 2000
**Number of employes in South Africa:** 550
**Products and services available in South Africa:** minicomputers and mainframes; storage systems; printers; terminals; punch card equipment; software, engineering support.

**SPERRY RAND CORPORATION**
1290 Avenue of the Americas
New York, NY 10019
**LOCAL SUBSIDIARY**
Sperry Univac
P.O. Box 5981
Johannesburg 2000

Number of employes in South Africa: 185
Products and services available in South Africa: a full spectrum of data processing equipment; storage systems; peripheral equipment; communications systems; multiplexers; computer-aided design systems; software; support.

IBM CORPORATION
Old Orchard Road
Armonk, NY 10504
**LOCAL SUBSIDIARY**
IBM South Africa (Pty.) Ltd.
P.O. Box 1419
Johannesburg 2000
Number of employes in South Africa: 1,460
Products and services available in South Africa: mini-, mid-range and mainframe computers; disk storage; tape drives; printers; terminals and other peripheral equipment; software; maintenance; consulting; training for industrial, commercial, scientific and academic users; computer bureau services; facsimile transmission equipment; computer-aided design equipment; encoders.

HEWLETT-PACKARD COMPANY
3200 Hillview Avenue
Palo Alto, CA 94304
**LOCAL SUBSIDIARY**
Hewlett Packard South Africa (Pty.) Ltd.
Private Bag Wendywood
Sandton 2144
Number of employes in South Africa: 97
Products and services available in South Africa: a full range of small and large computers; disk drives; printers; badge-readers; plastic card systems; software; computer-aided design equipment; training; consultant services; microprocessors.

NCR CORPORATION
Dayton, OH 45479
**LOCAL SUBSIDIARY**
NCR Corporation South Africa (Pty.) Ltd.
P.O. Box 3591
Johannesburg
Number of employes in South Africa: 830
Products and services available in South Africa: a full range of small and large computers; printers; terminals; disk storage; badge readers; encoders; modems; microprocessors; software; training.

MOHAWK DATA SCIENCES
1599 Littleton Road
Parsipanny, NJ 07054
**LOCAL SUBSIDIARY**
Mohawk Data Sciences South Africa (Pty.) Ltd.
P.O. Box 31281
Braamfontein 2017
**Number of employes in South Africa:** 80
**Products and services available in South Africa:** intelligent data capture systems; data communications equipment; peripheral processing equipment; software; microprocessors.


COMPUTER SCIENCES CORPORATION
650 North Sepulveda Boulevard
El Segundo, CA 90245
**LOCAL SUBSIDIARY**
Computer Sciences (Pty.) Ltd.
P.O. Box 31497
Braamfontein 2017
**Number of employes in South Africa:** 500
**Products and services available in South Africa:** sale and rental of minicomputers, terminals and locally manufactured equipment; computer bureau services; software; also markets equipment from Texas Instruments and ITT; electronic components.

Sources: "American Firms, Subsidiaries and Affiliates - South Africa September 1980", American Consulate, Johannesburg; *Computer Users Handbook*, 1980 and 1981.

# U.S. ELECTRONICS COMPANIES OPERATING THROUGH SOUTH AFRICAN DISTRIBUTORS

| Company | Parent Corporation (If Applicable) | South African Agent | Products Manufactured by Corporation |
|---|---|---|---|
| Apple Computer, Inc. Cupertino, CA | | Technetics (Pty) Ltd. | microcomputers |
| American Science and Engineering Inc. Cambridge, MA | | Fidelity Guards | micro-dose x-ray system for security systems |
| Boschert Inc. Sunnyvale, CA | | Technetics (Pty) Ltd. | switching power supplies |
| Braemer Computer Devices Inc. Burnsville, MN | | Infodata (Pty) Ltd. | cassette and mini-cassette tape drives, data loggers |
| Bendix Corp. Sidney, NY | | High Quality Electronic Components (Pty) Ltd. | electronic components |
| Bourns, Inc. Riverside, CA | | Associated Electronics | electronic components |
| Chromatics, Inc. Atlanta, GA | | Infodata (Pty) Ltd. | computer terminals |
| Centronics Data Computer Corp. Hudson, NY | | Anker Data Systems and Technetics (Pty) Ltd. | computer printers, teleprinters |
| Doculum Inc. Memphis, TN | | Identity and Laminating Services (Pty) Ltd. | employee identification instant photo I.D. system |
| Digital Equipment Corp. Maynard, MA | | Hurbarn Electronics (Pty) Ltd. | computers and peripheral equipment |

| Company | Parent Corporation (If Applicable) | South African Agent | Products Manufactured by Corporation |
|---------|------------------------------------|---------------------|--------------------------------------|
| Data 100 Corp. Minnetonka, MN | | Computer Sciences (Pty) Ltd. | computer terminals, miniconductors, and minicomputer systems |
| Data Terminal Systems, Inc. Maynard, MA | | Computer and Retail Equipment (Pty) Ltd. | not available |
| Epicom Inc. Altamonte Springs, FL | | General Data Systems | electronic instruments |
| Fairchild Industries Germantown, MD | | Altech | electronic components |
| Grinnell Corp. Providence, RI | ITT New York, NY | Infodata (Pty) Ltd. | not available |
| GTCO Corp. Rockville, MD | | Infodata (Pty) Ltd. | data processing machines |
| Houston Instruments Austin, TX | Bausch and Lomb Inc. Rochester, NY | Protea PNI (Pty) Ltd. | digital recorders, plotters, data processing and control systems computer peripheral equipment |
| Hypertronics Corp. Concord, MA | | Simark/Smith Industries | connectors |
| Hewlett-Packard Palo Alto, CA | | Fairmont Electronics (Pty) Ltd. | electronic components |
| Hazeltine Corp. Green Lawn, NY | | Anker Data Systems | video terminals, information electronics |
| Hendrix Electronics, Inc. Manchester, NH | | Photracomp | electronic equipment, editing displays |
| Integral Data Systems, Inc. Natich, MA | | Infodata (Pty) Ltd. | teleprinters |

| Company | Parent Corporation (If Applicable) | South African Agent | Products Manufactured by Corporation |
|---------|-----------------------------------|---------------------|--------------------------------------|
| Intelligent Systems Corp. | | Infodata (Pty) Ltd. | peripheral equipment |
| Imlac Corp. Needham, MA | Hazeltine Corp. Green Lawn, NY | Infodata (Pty) Ltd. | display terminals, detection and identification systems, electronic components |
| Information Terminals Corp. Sunnyvale, CA | | Advance Promotions (Pty) Ltd. | flexible disks, test instruments |
| Intel Corp. Santa Clara, CA | | Compower (Pty) Ltd. | computer memories |
| Micropolis Corp. Canoga Park, CA | | Radiokom (Pty) Ltd. | floppy disc drives |
| Mostek Corp. Carrolton, TX | United Technologies Corp. Hartford, CT | Radiokom (Pty) Ltd. | integrated circuits, semiconductor memories, logic products |
| Microdata Corp. Irvine, CA | McDonnell Douglas Corp. St. Louis, MO | Unicom (Pty) Ltd. | computers, magnetic recorders |
| Micom Systems, Inc. Chatsworth, CA | | General Data Systems | data communications systems |
| Motorola Inc. Schaumberg, IL | | Altech | electronic components |
| Nashua Corp. Nashua, NH | | Trident Computer Products (Pty) Ltd. | computer products, photo products |
| Okidata Corp. Mount Laurel, NJ | | Saco Systems (Pty) Ltd. | computer peripheral equipment |
| Ontel Corp. Woodbury, NY | Caesar's World Los Angeles, CA | Compower (Pty) Ltd. | intelligent computer terminals, minicomputers, software systems |

| Company | Parent Corporation (If Applicable) | South African Agent | Products Manufactured by Corporation |
|---|---|---|---|
| Printronix Inc. Irvine, CA | | Saco Systems (Pty) Ltd. | data printers |
| Qume Corp. San Jose, CA | ITT New York, NY | Technetics (Pty) Ltd. | electronic serial printers |
| Racal-Milgo Inc. Miami, FL | Racal Electronics Berks (UK) | General Data Systems | data communication systems |
| RCA Somerville, NJ | | Altech | electronic components |
| Scientific Micro Systems Mountain View, CA | Corning Glass Works Corning, NY | Technetics (Pty) Ltd. | microprogramming automation system |
| Summagraphics Corp. Fairfield, CT | | Protea PNI (Pty) Ltd. | computer peripheral equipment |
| Sanders Associates, Inc. Nashua, NH | | Infodata (Pty) Ltd. | electronic countermeasures equipment, graphics systems, computer microfilm printers |
| Siliconix Inc. Santa Clara, CA | Lucas Industries Birmingham, (UK) | Electrolink (Pty) Ltd. | electronic circuits transistors, semiconductors |
| Synertek Inc. Santa Clara, CA | Honeywell Inc. Minneapolis, MN | Radiokom (Pty) Ltd. | microprocessors, memory components and systems |
| Telonic/Berkeley Laguna Beach, CA | Berkeley Industries Inc. | Protea (Pty) Ltd. | test equipment, RF & microwave filters, alternators |
| Technipol International Corp. Foster City, CA | | IIAS (Pty) Ltd. | equipment and training techniques for law enforcement and security agencies worldwide |

| Company | Parent Corporation (If Applicable) | South African Agent | Products Manufactured by Corporation |
|---|---|---|---|
| TRW Inc. Cleveland, OH | | Electrolink (Pty) Ltd. | electronics components aerospace computers, systems and services |
| Technetics, Inc. El Cajon, CA | | Semiconductor Control Systems (Pty) Ltd. | electronic test equipment |
| Unitrode Corp. Lexington, MA | | Electrolink (Pty) Ltd. | semiconductors, diodes, rectifiers |
| Verbatim Corp. Sunnyvale, CA | | Advance Promotions (Pty) Ltd. | magnetic discs |
| VRN International Division St. Petersburg, FL | Vernitron Corp. Lake Success, NY | Electrolink (Pty) Ltd. | potentiometers |
| Versatec Santa Clara, CA | Xerox Corp. Stamford, CT | Photracomp | computer peripheral equipment, printers, plotters, plotting software |
| Westinghouse Electric Corp. Pittsburgh, PA | | Altech | electronic components |

SOURCES:
*Directory of Corporate Affiliations; Electronics Buyer's Guide; Electronics and Instrumentation*, Johannesburg, July, 1979; *Electronics and Instrumentation*, Johannesburg, Sept., 1979; *Financial Times*, London, Nov. 28, 1980; *Security and Protection of South Africa*, Johannesburg, Oct. 1980; *The South African Computer User's Handbook*, Braamfontein, 1980; *Standard and Poor's Million Dollar Directory; Thomas Register; Who Owns Whom* — North America.

# U.S. COMPUTER SUPPORT FOR WHITE-CONTROLLED REGIONAL AND LOCAL AGENCIES

| Government Body | Hardware | Origin |
|---|---|---|
| Alberton Municipality | Century 100 | National Cash Register (NCR) |
| Bloemfontein Municipality | Criterion 8500 | NCR |
| Boksburg Municipality | Model 9030 | Sperry Univac |
| King Williamstown Municipality | Century 100 | NCR |
| Brakpan Municipality | Model 101 | NCR |
| Brits Municipality | Model 34 | IBM |
| Cape Divisional Council | Model 2200T | Wang |
| Cape Provincial Administration | Model 1120; Model 1130 | Sperry Univac IBM |
| Cape Town Municipality | Model 5500 | Datapoint |
| Durban Municipality | Model 2200 Two Minicomputers | Wang Honeywell |
| Ermelo Municipality | Model 1700 | Burroughs |
| Fochville Municipality | Two Model 299s | NCR |
| Germiston Municipality | Model 360/30 Model 1200 | IBM Mohawk |
| Johannesburg Municipality | Model 2410 Model 3 | Mohawk Nova |
| Kempton Park Municipality | Century 200 | NCR |
| Kingsburgh Municipality | Model 2200 | Wang |
| Kokstad Municipality | Model 8250 | NCR |
| Louis Trichard Municipality | Models 8250 and 8230 | NCR |
| Middleburg Municipality | Model 3 | Nova |
| Natal Province | Model 2200 | Wang |
| Newcastle Municipality | Model 3/150 | IBM |
| Orange Free State Province | Model 1204 | Mohawk |
| Oudtshoorn Municipality | Model 8230 | NCR |
| Parow Municipality | Century 200 | NCR |
| Pretoria Peri-Urban Areas Board | Model 3/15 | IBM |

| Government Body | Hardware | Origin |
|---|---|---|
| Pietersburg Municipality | Century 100 | NCR |
| Pinetown Municipality | Model 34 | IBM |
| Port Elizabeth Divisional Council | NA | Wang |
| Randburg Municipality | Model 1726 | Burroughs |
| Randfontein Municipality | Models 10/158 and 1403 | IBM |
| Richards Bay Municipality | Model 3/8 | IBM |
| Rustenburg Municipality | Century 151 | NCR |
| Sandton Municipality | Model 1860 | Burroughs |
| Somerset West Municipality | Century 100 | NCR |
| Stanger Municipality | Model 34 | IBM |
| Stellenbosch Divisional Council | Century 200 | NCR |
| Stellenbosch Municipality | Century 100 | NCR |
| Tongaat Municipality | Model 2200T | Wang |
| Transvaal Province | Model 6700 | Burroughs |
| Tzaneen Municipality | Model 100 | NCR |
| Vanderbijlpark Municipality | Model 3500 | Burroughs |
| Walvis Bay Municipality | Model 8200 | NCR |
| Westville Municipality | Model 32 | IBM |
| Witbank Municipality | Criterion 8450 and Century 100 | NCR |
| Worcester Municipality | Century 101 | NCR |

SOURCES: *SA Computer Users Handbook 1980* and *Electronics and Instrumentation.*

# U.S. COMPUTER INSTALLATIONS AT CENTRAL GOVERNMENT AGENCIES AND STATE-OWNED CORPORATIONS

| Hardware | User |
|---|---|
| Data General Nova 2 | Department of Justice |
| IBM 370; 370/155 | Atomic Energy Board |
| IBM 370/155; 3 Mohawk 2402s | Department of Inland Revenue |
| IBM 370/158 | Human Science Research Council |
| IBM 370 | Department of the Prime Minister |
| IBM 360 | Department of Statistics |
| Control Data Cyber 174 and 175; Cyber 720; Wang 2200 PCS | Electricity Supply Commission |
| IBM 3/10; 34; IBM Model 6 Wang Minicomputer | Industrial Development Corporation |
| Sperry Univac 1100/12 | South African Reserve Bank |
| Two IBM 370s | Department of the Interior |
| IBM 370/158 | Department of Education |
| Datapoint 5500 | Department of Trade |
| Mohawk 2404 | Department of Treasury |
| Varian V76; V72; 29 2200s; Six Datapoint 5500s | Department of Water Affairs |
| Data General Nova 3; Nova 1200 | Phosphate Development Corporation |
| Control Data Cyber 74; 3500; 31/70; 720; Burroughs 1955; 7800; Ontel and Prime | South Africa Iron and Steel Industrial Corporation |
| Burroughs B821 | NAMASCOR |
| 88 Data General Novas; IBM | South African Railways |
| Sperry Univac 1110; 1106 | South African Coal, Oil and Gas Corporation |
| Foxboro 1/2 | Uranium Enrichment Corporation |
| Burroughs B3500; B3700 | Union Steel Corporation |
| IBM 370/158; IBM 4331 | Vecor Heavy Engineering |

| Hardware | User |
|---|---|
| Data General Nova 3 | SAFAIR Freighters |
| IBM 3/15 | African Metals Corporation |
| IBM 370/158; IBM 370/3032; IBM 370/168 | South African Airways |
| NCR 8230 | SAPEKO |
| Wang 2200 | Southern Oil Exploration Corporation |
| Datapoint 2200; 3360; 5500 | Durban Navigational Collieries |
| Datapoint 6600 Arc System | Klipfontein Organic Products |
| Texas Instruments; Data General Eclipse; PDP; Nova 820; NCR 8430 | National Institute for Metallurgy |

Note: This list does not include installations at the CSIR, police and military installations and others outlined with more detail in the text.

Sources: *National Register of Service Rendering Information Centres and of Data Banks; Computer Users Handbook 1980; U.S. Business in South Africa - The Economic, Political and Moral Issues.*

## SALES OF EQUIPMENT MADE BY U.S. ELECTRONICS AND COMPUTER COMPANIES THROUGH THE STATE TENDER BOARD

| U.S. Maker | Awarding South African Agency or Department of Record | Date of Announcement |
| --- | --- | --- |
| Perkin-Elmer | State Purchases | September 26, 1980 |
| Hivac | AL | October 3, 1980 |
| Kodak | Posts and Telecommunications | October 3, 1980 |
| 3M | State Purchases | October 3, 1980 |
| Hewlett-Packard | Posts and Telecommunications | October 3, 1980 |
| Hewlett-Packard | Posts and Telecommunications | November 7, 1980 |
| Bell and Howell | Water Affairs | November 7, 1980 |
| Hewlett-Packard | State Purchases | November 7, 1980 |
| RCA | State Purchases | November 7, 1980 |
| Hewlett-Packard | Posts and Telecommunications | December 5, 1980 |
| Bell and Howell | State Purchases | December 12, 1980 |
| Bell and Howell | State Purchases | January 16, 1981 |
| 3M | Not available | January 9, 1981 |
| Hewlett-Packard | State Purchases | January 9, 1981 |
| Rockwell | Public Works | January 23, 1981 |
| 3M | Not available | January 23, 1981 |
| Apple Computers | Posts and Telecommunications | January 23, 1981 |
| General Electric | Posts and Telecommunications | January 23, 1981 |
| Hewlett-Packard | State Purchases | January 30, 1981 |
| Fairchild | State Purchases | February 6, 1981 |
| ITT | State Purchases | February 6, 1981 |
| Hewlett-Packard | Posts and Telecommunications | February 13, 1981 |
| Hewlett-Packard | Posts and Telecommunications | February 20, 1981 |
| Hewlett-Packard | State Purchases | February 27, 1981 |
| Motorola | State Purchases | February 27, 1981 |
| Data General | State Purchases | February 27, 1981 |
| Centronics/ Printronics | State Purchases | March 13, 1981 |

Source: *State Tender Bulletin*

# BACKGROUND ON CSIR AFFILIATES ENGAGED IN MILITARY WORK

Following is a description of the major CSIR laboratories and affiliates that perform military-related R&D or consulting services.

## • National Institute for Defense Research (NIDR)

Located in Pretoria, the National Institute for Defense Research (NIDR) pioneered in guided missile research in the '60s, collaborating with two ARMSCOR subsidiaries on the Cactus missile.[1] Fullscale production of the Cactus has been taken over by ARMSCOR, but the NIDR has continued its military work. The few published accounts of Institute work, which have appeared in South African engineering journals, indicate that the NIDR has access to sophisticated arms development technology. For example, the Institute maintains three dedicated digital simulation facilities used for testing and designing missiles at several phases of their development and production.[2] The NIDR also conducts actual flight trials at a missile testing range at an undisclosed site.

NIDR scientists have been devoting increasing attention to advanced electronics, the basis of most modern weaponry. In a 1980 paper entitled "Application of Digital Signal Processing to Military Systems" one of the Institute's researchers outlined the use of charge-coupled devices in moving target indication radar.[3] Another publication indicates NIDR's interest in the application of acoustic wave devices to electronic countermeasures and ground-to-air communications.[4]

The Institute quietly parcels out research contracts to trusted outside agencies. In 1980, one researcher at the University of Stellenbosch reported on contract work he had performed for the NIDR, concerning applications of microwave filters.[5]

In 1974, the NIDR was on record as using several U.S. computers supplied by Varian, a company which has since been acquired by Sperry.[6] Despite the NIDR's contribution to South Africa's arsenal, the U.S. Commerce Department has decided that most exports to the Institute will not be prohibited. In defiance of logic, the Department stated that it "does not consider the National Institute for Defense Research (NIDR) to be a military entity, because it does research for private as well as military organizations," according to a Commerce regulation.[7] Exports to the NIDR are prohibited by the Commerce Department only if the exporter *knows* the product is intended for a specific military project.

- **National Institute for Aeronautics and Systems Technology (NIAST)**

The NIAST performs strategic R&D in the field of aeronautics for South Africa's aviation industry, the major emphasis of which is the manufacture of military aircraft for the air force.[8] The government suppresses details about NIAST's work because of its military applications and the agency does not publish an annual report, unlike many other CSIR subsidiaries. However, the CSIR has disclosed that the main activities of the Institute involve flight dynamics, aerodynamics, aircraft structures, propulsion, servomechanisms and digital and microwave systems.[9] Computer technology apparently plays a key role in the work of the Institute. Researchers there use CAD/CAM (computer-aided design/computer-aided manufacturing) techniques.[10]

NIAST researchers have direct access to the central Control Data installation at the CSIR computing center in Pretoria. NIAST also uses a model 7/32 supplied by Perkin-Elmer, another U.S. corporation.[11]

- **National Research Institute for Mathematical Sciences (NRIMS)**

Located in Pretoria, the NRIMS conducts basic and applied mathematical research. Work on optimization theory and applications is a major focus of the Institute and in 1979, Control Data Corporation gave a grant to NRIMS to support research in this field. IBM also subsidized the Institute with a grant the same year.

In addition to these subsidies and the Institute's use of U.S. computer technology, NRIMS has substantial contacts with U.S. experts. For example, a South African scientist, who now works at IBM's Watson Research Center in the United States, lectured at the Institute in September of 1979, followed by another researcher from the University of California, who spent two and one-half months there. At least four members of the Institute visited the United States on official business during 1979 and 1980. Details of their contacts in the United States were published in internal Institute reports.

The NRIMS provides consulting services to other government agencies and performs a range of contract research. Many of the Institute's larger projects involve sensitive work and are "of a confidential nature," because of their military and internal security applications. For instance, one branch of the Institute works on computer graphics for image processing, a field with numerous military applications. Another Institute researcher, M. King, designed a sophisticated system for fingerprint storage. The Institute is also researching connections between handwriting and personality. Late in 1979, NRIMS worked on a military contract for Infoplan concerning target acquisition, followed in 1980 by another Infoplan project. Other Institute projects in 1980, included contract work for the NIAST and a computer-aided design program for Lyttleton Engineering Works, a major ARMSCOR subsidiary.[12]

- **The National Mechanical Engineering Research Institute (NMERI) and the National Chemical Research Laboratory (NCRL)**

Both of these organizations, which have access to the IBM/Control Data computer network, perform military-related work on a contract basis, including projects for the South African air force, ordnance development and metallurgical testing. In 1980, for example, the NCRL provided consulting services to the Hoedspruit Air Force Base. In addition to the CSIR computers, NCRL scientists have access to a Hewlett-Packard computer.

In 1980, according to a report from the NMERI, researchers there worked on a project to develop a new design for explosive shells. In another project to test the impact of nearby explosions on vehicles, the Institute developed a "Shock Response Spectrum" with a Varian computer which was plotted on the Control Data mainframe at the CSIR. Scientists at the Institute are helping South Africa beat the arms embargo, which has dried up access to certain military parts.[13] In 1979, the Institute made a breakthrough in the development of a new prototype glass fiber helicopter blade to replace foreign imports.[14] NMERI also maintains a large 7-meter wind tunnel for aerodynamic testing, according to the Institute's annual report.

- **The National Accelerator Center (NAC), Pretoria Cyclotron Group and the Atomic Energy Board (AEB)**

The NAC and the Pretoria Cyclotron Group serve as research and training facilities for South Africa's growing nuclear industry. The Cyclotron Group also produces radioactive isotopes. In addition to their own computers, both of these facilities have access to the main Control Data/IBM installation at the CCS.[15]

The Atomic Energy Board, though not a subsidiary of the CSIR, oversees much of the nuclear work in South Africa, and has acquired sensitive technology from a U.S.-owned company. A West German subsidiary of Sperry has supplied precision instruments to the AEB that are critical to uranium enrichment. South Africa is now able to produce nuclear weapons, it is generally believed, and access to foreign uranium enrichment technology has helped make it possible for Pretoria to manufacture modest quantities of bomb-grade material.

In 1979, an official of Varian-MAT, a small firm in Bremen, West Germany that is owned by Sperry, confirmed that the company had exported to South Africa a computer-based mass spectrometer system that is "exclusively constructed" for use in enrichment plants.[16] The revelation came in the course of a national TV program, *Monitor*, aired late in November. The system was ordered by National Chemical Products, on behalf of the AEB, according to the company representative. Although Varian-MAT is owned by a U.S. corporation, the transaction escaped public attention in the United States because the equipment was shipped from German soil.[17]

• **The National Electrical Engineering Research Institute (NEERI)**

With substantial links to the South African military establishment and key defense contractors, the CSIR's National Electrical Engineering Research Institute (NEERI) is making great strides in the development of advanced electronics for Pretoria. The involvement of several military officials and corporate representatives with the Institute underscores the value of NEERI's work for the war effort. Among them are F.J. Bell, a senior manager in the External Production Division of ARMSCOR; W.A. Brading, a technical director with Standard Telephone and Cables (SA), Ltd.; Commodore P.L. Nolte, Director of Military Engineering for the SADF; A.G. Marshall, an executive with Plessey (SA), Ltd.; Major General D.G. van Niekerk, Chief of Air Staff Logistics, SADF; D.H. Botha, manager of the Telecommunications, Radar and Computers Group at ARMSCOR; and Colonel C.R. Labuschagne, of the Signal Projects division, SADF.

Despite these connections and NEERI's military work, U.S. computer and electronics suppliers are apparently not prohibited from doing business with the Institute. In addition to NEERI's access to the Control Data and IBM computers at the CSIR, the Institute uses hardware supplied by Digital Equipment Corporation and Calcomp, both U.S. corporations.

Other contacts between U.S. corporations and the Institute suggest an even closer relationship. In the spring and summer of 1980, NEERI research officers participated in two seminars held in South Africa by Hewlett-Packard and Fluke, a U.S. corporation which markets measuring devices. A published list of visitors to the Institute indicates that a scientist from Westinghouse Electric Corporation and a "Mr. E. Mount," a director of GE from the United States, were both guests at NEERI on an undisclosed date.

Virtually all NEERI's contract work is "of a confidential nature." The Institute's major contributions to the military-industrial complex have been the establishment of a small specialized integrated circuit production facility; research in large-scale integrated circuits; work in signal processing; and development of computer-aided design programs.[18]

• **National Institute for Telecommunications Research (NITR)**

The NITR performs longterm R&D in radio communications, according to its 1980 annual report. As the Institute points out, a great deal of its work "is directly in the national interest and concerns both the future prosperity of the country and the immediate needs of certain government and semi-government departments." Much of this work, says the Institute, is "classified as it relates to defense." Representatives from ARMSCOR, the Telecommunications Office of the South African army and from local military electronics firms help oversee NITR work, which is carried out at headquarters in Johannesburg and at three other sites.

U.S. computers are vital to the work of the National Institute for Telecommunications Research, which is linked to the Control Data and IBM computer facility at the CSIR's Centre for Computing Services.[19] The Institute also relies on its own hardware system, which includes an IBM 1130, and six Hewlett-Packard units in the 2100 range.[20] The NITR has played an integral role in the development of South Africa's air defense system, according to one senior military scientist.[21] NITR also provides regular forecasts of optimum radio traffic frequencies to the defence force, and "various government departments," and plans to expand its work on high frequency communications.

The NITR operates a satellite remote sensing center at Hartebeesthoek in cooperation with NASA. About 30 km north of Pretoria, the Institute also maintains another satellite tracking facility in conjunction with the French National Space Agency. Two members of the Institute participate in space research projects at the University of Michigan, according to NITR's annual report for 1980.

• **National Physical Research Laboratory (NPRL)**

The NPRL is engaged in a wide range of research, including non-strategic work and R&D "in the national interest." In conjunction with the NITR, the Laboratory operates a radar facility at Houtkoppen. NPRL scientists also do applied research in the optical sciences, high-pressure physics, acoustics and other fields. During 1979, NPRL facilities were at the disposal of several ARMSCOR subsidiaries and other military producers. The Laboratory's Precise Physical Measurements Division rendered consulting services to several arms makers which are listed in the table below.

| Producer | Specialty Area |
| --- | --- |
| Atlas Aircraft | military aircraft and maintenance |
| Kentron | guided missile design and manufacture |
| Eloptro | military electro-optics |
| Atomic Energy Board | nuclear research |
| Cementation Engineering | ordnance development |
| Naschem | explosives, propellants and ammunition |
| NIAST | aerospace technology |
| Pretoria Metal Pressings | ammunition |
| Marconi | telecommunications |
| Transronic | communications |
| Dorman Long | shipbuilding |
| Plessey | electronics |

The NPRL also established a metallurgical laboratory for the South African air force, and helped outfit it with technology acquired from overseas.

In addition to the Laboratory's access to the U.S. computer system at the CSIR central facility, NPRL uses other U.S. technology, including two atomic absorption spectrometers from Perkin-Elmer and Varian, and computers from Digital Equipment Corporation, Motorola and Hewlett-Packard.

The links between the NPRL and U.S. multinationals go beyond the supply of hardware. In 1979, for example, a representative of NPRL visited the West German facility of a Sperry subsidiary, Varian-MAT, the same corporation that has done business with the South African Atomic Energy Board.

Late in 1979, George Olsen, a senior scientist at the RCA Laboratories in Princeton, New Jersey, participated in a colloquium at the NPRL. Olsen reported on the fabrication of semiconductors for electro-optical applications.[22] Part of Olsen's work in this field was conducted for and paid by the U.S. Department of Defense Advanced Research Projects Agency (DARPA) in Arlington, Virginia.[23] Olsen has also worked on other military electronics projects for DARPA, for RCA and the U.S. Army Electronics Command.[24] In addition, NPRL has performed contract work in the field of laser technology for Tachisto, a small privately-held electronics firm based in Massachusetts which has done work for the U.S. Department of Defense.[25]